RETRO DINER

Comfort Food from the American Roadside

LINDA EVERETT

PORTLAND, OREGON

Library of Congress Cataloging-in-Publication Data

Everett, Linda, 1946–
    Retro diner : comfort food from the American roadside / by Linda
Everett.
        p. cm.
    ISBN 1-888054-68-9 (Hardcover)
    1. Cookery, American. 2. Diners (Restaurants)–United States. I. Title.
    TX715 .E9213 2002
        641.5973–dc21

                                                2002005729

Design: Trina Stahl
Editor: Brenda Koplin

Printed in Singapore
9 8 7 6

Contents

Introduction

Through a long and colorful history diner-style restaurants have brought rib-sticking, taste bud-satisfying comfort food to hungry Americans. Their beginnings were simple sandwich carts parked across from mills and factories where they fed weary blue-collar workers. Soon they expanded in size and design to the sleek stainless steel portable diners we think of today.

When fast food and even faster highways bypassed these American icons, their future looked bleak and many disappeared into the scrap heap. After decades there was a resurgence in the glow of the 1950s good life. The appeal of tasteless, preformed 'burgers n' fries at the interstate off-ramp lost its excitement. Travelers, locals, and families alike rediscovered honest flavorful food, coupled with good service and a homey atmosphere, at the corner diner.

Retro Diner is a fun fifties-style view of diners and the comfort food we remember. Forget the tofu and twigs and browse through recipes for Roman Holiday Soup, Sugar Baby Slaw, and, of course, Mom's Meat Loaf. We won't tell. Accompanying these all-American

recipes are bits of grill-side lore for a light-hearted sit-at-the-counter kind of read. Here's the waitress, who remembers your name, with your coffee and a slice of Foot High Meringue Pie. You're back in the fifties when Elvis is on the jukebox, Eisenhower makes us feel like a family, and food is cooked from scratch with pride and care.

HOW IT ALL BEGAN

The American diner began as a product of the great industrial revolution in Providence, Rhode Island, sometime around 1872. At that time even factory towns rolled up their sidewalks when the sun went down. Overworked laborers on the swing shift had to be satisfied with a cold bucket lunch because no decent eateries were open at those late hours. An entrepreneurial man, Walter Scott, took his horse-drawn wagon, cut holes in the canvas sides for windows, and sold sandwiches, slices of homemade pie, and

steaming coffee to the hungry workers. Soon, these "wagons" were popping up on street corners around the country.

By the turn of the century lunch wagons were making the shift from shabby horse carts or retired trolley cars to structures distinctively all their own. Although many nonaficionados still believe diners were recycled railroad dining cars, the only real connection is the name diner. The blueprint for authentic diners did borrow a few ideas from gleaming railroad cars, but they evolved into a creation all their own. Soon several factories were riveting together their custom-made products under picturesque names like Jerry O'Mahony, Bixler, Paramount, Monarchs, Kullman Dining Car Company, Worcester, and Mountain View. Prices ranged from $30,000 to $150,000 for one with all the sparkles including jukeboxes, cigarette machines, and toothpick dispensers. Some companies boasted that they made two entire diners per day, ready to be moved to that street corner or highway intersection. By the 1950s there were more than six thousand across the U.S.A. offering everything from full-course meals to those simple hot dogs.

Somehow, diners managed to survive the ravages of the Great Depression, but as smoking mills and belching factories were closed and turned to rust heaps, they suffered. By the late 1960s many classic diners, beauties made of sleek, aerodynamically designed steel and porcelain, were gone. Some owners attempted to remodel into the modern look—the gleaming quilted stainless steel covered by colonial brick or space-age additions—anything to make the diner look up-to-date and more like a Denny's or other chain restaurant.

Some neighborhood diners have managed to cruise along through the ebb and flow of fads and popularity. The clientele has transformed from mill and factory workers to CEOs, the local choir after rehearsal, computer techies, tourists, and families. Typical are the ones like the Capitol in Lynn, Massachusetts, run by generations of the same family for the past fifty years, or O'Rourke's in Middletown, Connecticut, which has been in the family for fifty-three years. At O'Rourke's everything is made fresh daily right down to the sauces, soups, bread, and potato chips. The proud owner starts work at 2:00 A.M. and opens at 4:30 A.M. to catch workers or fishermen. These diners stay in business and weather economic storms because they offer great food and equally good service.

By the late 1970s and early 1980s a few outside boosts kept diners in the public eye. The movies *Diner, Tin Men*, and *Goodfellas* all featured diners as the new, nifty place to meet. TV shows caught the baby boomers' interest with "Happy Days," "Laverne and Shirley," and "Alice." The '50s were now looking like the golden years, the uncomplicated era when you could solve your latest boyfriend problem over a 'burger and fries at Mel's. A few glitzy pseudo-diners (or "Disney diners" according to traditional diner-philes) popped up to catch the nostalgia wave. The retro-chic trendy Empire Diner on 10th Avenue in New York City and the Fog City Diner in San Francisco made their bid to revive the age.

Fresh . . .
STRAWBERRY SHORT CAKE
Topped with
WHIPPED CREAM
m-m-m--good!

Call it a resurgence, or perhaps just a long past-due appreciation of diners, their style, and their ambience, but enthusiasm is growing. The Japanese and some Europeans are paying six- and seven-figure prices for classic, restored diner gems. Maybe they haven't a clue about the decidedly nondiner-quality food, but they must feel cool in their studded leather jackets, sitting in red upholstered booths with their imported Harleys at the curb.

Look around the country, mostly in the Northeast, and you'll find more than two thousand Kullmans, O'Mahonys, Sterlings, and Worcesters—some as small as O'Rourke's with eleven booths and an L-shaped counter that seats fifteen. Waitresses still check that mirrored ceiling to see if you need a refill on your cuppa joe. And the closeness of the stools at the counter works like its own United Nations. The patrons are gently urged to start conversations with their solely American-type of friendliness and familiarity. Oh, not all diners order up the perfect pot pie or mouthwatering meat loaf, but chances are if you see a line outside the door and the curbside full, you can bet there's something worth the wait inside that quilted stainless steel exterior. This is everybody's place.

Diners have forever been there for the early riser. Originally these corner eateries fed the early factory worker on the way to a tough job where hearty food—and plenty of it—fueled a long day on the assembly line. The diner doors always opened before the sun was even a hint in the morning sky, with the coffee brewing hot and strong.

As factories shut down over the years, the breakfast crowd changed in most of the diner neighborhoods, but the "open" sign is still there at first light. Perhaps now the customers are different, but the welcoming all-American breakfast is pretty much the same. Many classic diners have a long line of regulars, mostly families, waiting on Sunday mornings for their weekly meal of Lucy's Diner's Golden Waffles, a stack of Bald Mountain Diner's Griddle Cakes (a classic 1938 recipe), or that delectable tender Country Omelets from Patty Patty's. This is the place where Americans can begin their day.

Mile High Biscuits

2 cups sifted flour
2$^{1}/_{2}$ tsps baking powder
1 tsp salt
$^{1}/_{3}$ cup shortening (or real
    butter makes wonderful
    flavor)
$^{2}/_{3}$ cup milk, more or less

1. Preheat oven to 425 degrees.

2. Sift flour, baking powder, and salt into a medium bowl.

3. Blend in shortening or butter. Although there are nifty little tools to use for blending, like a pastry cutter, I prefer crumbling with my fingers. Keep this up until the mixture looks like coarse cornmeal.

4. Stir in milk with a fork, a little at a time until dough is soft but not sticky.

5. Dump onto a lightly floured board or clean counter and knead about 20 times.

6. Roll dough out until it's about 1-inch thick. Cut with a floured biscuit cutter or floured rim of small glass. Avoid handling dough too much because that makes it tough.

7. Place biscuits about 1 inch apart on an ungreased baking sheet and bake 12 to 15 minutes. Keep a close watch on them because all ovens are a bit different and they may scorch. I figure they're done when the top is a delicate golden brown.

8. Serve generously with that homemade jam or preserves or local honey (I get mine as a Christmas present from a ranch in eastern Oregon), or split in half and smother with luscious thick gravy (see page 24).

Biscuits Supreme

2 cups all-purpose flour
4 tsps baking powder
$^{1}/_{2}$ tsp salt
$^{1}/_{2}$ tsp cream of tartar
2 tsp sugar
$^{1}/_{2}$ cup shortening
$^{2}/_{3}$ cup milk

1. Prepare the same as Mile High Biscuits, adding the cream of tarter and sugar at the same time as the baking powder. These are lighter, fluffier, and sweeter.

Hunter's Crescent Rolls

Start this the night before your celebration or get-together.

1 package yeast
¼ cup warm water
½ cup sugar
2 sticks good baking margarine
1 cup milk
2 eggs
4 cups all-purpose flour or bread flour

THIS RECIPE WAS generously shared by the wife of a hunter and logger. When hunting time rolled around she'd pack a lunch for her hubby and stuff in a bagful of these rolls. No matter how squashed and battered they got they still tasted wonderful. I highly recommend making a double batch at holiday time because everyone will want to take some home and you'll want leftovers.

1. Soften yeast in warm water, set aside.

2. In a large bowl beat together sugar and margarine.

3. Add milk and eggs.

4. Slowly mix in flour and yeast until smooth.

5. Refrigerate overnight.

6. The next day preheat oven to 375 degrees.

7. Divide dough into fifths. Roll each section into a round shape about ¼-inch thick.

8. Divide each of these "pies" into eighths, like cutting a pie.

9. Roll each triangular-shaped piece from the large end to the small, tucking the end underneath.

10. Bake until lightly browned, about 12 minutes.

11. Serve with your favorite preserves, jam, or honey.

Sinful Biscuits

4 cups sifted self-rising flour
1/2 cup lard (okay! I know
    it's dreadful because of
    cholesterol, but nothing
    else works for the flavor
    and texture)
1 1/3 cups milk

1. Preheat oven to 450 degrees.

2. In a large mixing bowl pour in flour and cut in lard. Use a pastry blender or your fingers, mixing until the consistency of coarse cornmeal.

3. Pour in milk and mix with a fork until dough forms a ball.

4. Turn dough out on a lightly floured board and knead about five times.

5. Roll out to about 1/2-inch thick and cut with biscuit cutter or floured rim of small glass.

6. Place about 1 inch apart on ungreased baking sheet.

7. Bake about 15 minutes.

8. Again, serve with your favorite jelly, jam, preserves, marmalade, or local honey (it has more flavor than the store-bought kind). Enjoy!

Get Your Roughage Bran Muffins

1/2 cup all-purpose flour
1 tsp baking powder
1/4 tsp salt
2 tblsps nonfat dry milk
1/2 cup whole-bran cereal
1 egg
1/4 cup water
1/2 tsp sugar
1 tblsp vegetable oil
1/4 cup raisins

1. Preheat oven to 400 degrees.

2. Sift together flour, baking powder, and salt in a medium bowl.

3. Stir in dry milk and cereal.

4. In a separate bowl beat together egg, water, sugar, and oil.

5. Stir wet mixture into dry until all is moist. Add raisins.

6. Spoon into greased muffin cups and bake 20 to 25 minutes.

7. Slurp on some real butter with a dab of local honey, and yum!

Dairyland Rolls

3/4 cup milk
1/2 cup shortening
1/2 cup sugar
1 tsp salt
2 packages active dry yeast
1/2 cup warm water (110 to
   115 degrees)
4 1/4 to 4 3/4 cups sifted
   white flour
2 eggs
1/4 cup melted butter

1. In a medium saucepan scald the milk; add in the shortening, sugar and salt.

2. Cool to lukewarm.

3. In a separate small bowl sprinkle yeast on the warm water.

4. Add 1 1/2 cups flour to the milk mixture; beat well by hand or with a mixer on low speed for 1 minute.

5. Beat in eggs and yeast.

6. Gradually stir in enough of the remaining flour, a few tablespoons at a time, until it makes a soft dough.

7. Turn onto a lightly floured board and knead until smooth, about 5 to 8 minutes. Dough should be shiny and no longer sticky.

8. Lightly grease a large bowl and turn dough into it.

9. Cover and let rise in a warm place until doubled in size, about 1 to 1 1/2 hours.

10. Punch down and turn back onto the floured board. Divide into rolls and place in shallow baking pan.

11. Brush tops lightly with melted butter and let rise until doubled once again. This will take about 30 to 40 minutes.

12. Bake in 400 degrees for 12 to 15 minutes, or until golden brown.

13. Makes about 30 rolls.

TOO MUCH SHORTENING UNFAIR TO YEAST

Indiana Buckwheat Cakes

1 egg
1¼ cups buttermilk, divided
(you can also use sweet
milk with 1 tsp white
vinegar added)
½ cup buckwheat flour
½ cup all-purpose white flour
½ tsp Salt
½ tsp baking soda
2 tblsps sugar
½ tsp baking powder
2 tblsps melted butter
butter for frying

1. In a small bowl beat together egg and 1 cup buttermilk.

2. In a medium-sized bowl mix together buckwheat and white flour, salt, baking soda, and sugar.

3. Make a well in flour mixture and pour in egg and milk mixture. Stir long enough only to moisten thoroughly.

4. Gently stir in melted butter.

5. Add up to ¼ cup of reserved buttermilk if batter is too thick to pour easily. Batter should be the consistency of heavy cream.

6. Warm your griddle on medium heat and melt 1 tblsp of the butter for frying.

7. Pour out 'cakes in 6-inch diameter. (I make my grandsons "mouse" pancakes with one large 'cake topped by two smaller "ears.")

8. Flip when top is covered in popping bubbles, about 3 to 5 minutes. 'Cakes should be light golden brown. Serve immediately because they lose something when kept warm in the oven.

9. Serve with your favorite syrup (real maple is worth the extra cost), a fruity syrup such as blackberry, apricot, or blueberry, try some of grandma's preserves, or pour on that wonderful honey.

Frenchie's Breakfast Toast

3 large eggs (if you want to
go thin use 1 whole egg
and 2 whites)

¹/₄ cup half and half (use
skim milk if you feel
guilty)

¹/₂ tsp ground cinnamon

¹/₂ tsp ground nutmeg

¹/₂ tsp vanilla extract

8 1-inch-thick pieces of
French bread, or
experiment with raisin
or other tasty breads

butter (or nonstick spray)

powdered sugar

1. Preheat oven to 200 degrees.

2. In a shallow bowl whisk together eggs until foamy.

3. Add in half and half, spices, and vanilla. Beat well.

4. Melt enough butter to coat the bottom of your skillet.

5. Dip pieces of bread in egg-milk mixture and cook in skillet on medium heat until golden brown. Turn once, cooking about 2 minutes on each side. Be sure not to let the butter burn.

6. As slices cook, place on a heatproof plate and keep warm in the oven.

7. Sprinkle lightly with powdered sugar and serve with your favorite syrup: maybe real maple, blueberry, or homemade preserves. Honey is also a good choice.

BREAKFASTS

(Please Order by Number)

No. 1
2 HOT CAKES WITH HAM,
BACON OR SAUSAGE,
AND I EGG 85c

No. 2
HAM, BACON OR SAUSAGE
TWO EGGS, POTATOES
AND TOAST 95c

No. 3
TWO HOT CAKES WITH
TWO EGGS 75c

No. 4
HAM, BACON OR SAUSAGE,
ONE EGG, POTATOES
AND TOAST 85c

No. 5
TWO EGGS, ANY STYLE, WITH
TOAST AND POTATOES 65c

No. 6
TWO HOT CAKES, WITH HAM,
BACON OR SAUSAGE 75c

No. 7
FRUIT OR CEREAL, WITH
TOAST AND JELLY 50c

No. 8
STEAK AND EGGS, WITH
POTATOES, TOAST AND
JELLY 1.25

——DRINKS EXTRA——

——SIDE ORDERS——

HAM, BACON or
SAUSAGE

POTATOES 25c
TWO EGGS

Jim Scarborough's Cornbread

2 cups cornmeal
1/4 cup sugar
1 tsp salt
2 eggs, well beaten
2 cups sweet milk, divided
4 tblsps butter
1 cup sour milk with 1 tsp
    baking soda (you can
    use buttermilk or whole
    milk with 1 tsp white
    vinegar added, but you'll
    still need the soda)

1. Preheat oven to 350 degrees.

2. In a large mixing bowl beat together cornmeal, sugar, salt, eggs, 1 cup sweet milk, and sour milk with soda.

3. In a 12-inch (or so) cast-iron skillet melt butter. Swirl pan around to cover sides.

4. Pour in batter, then pour 1 cup sweet milk over all. Do not stir!

5. Bake 1 hour. Test by poking a clean butter knife in the center. If it comes out clean it's done.

6. Serve with some of that prized jam, preserves, or local honey.

Bald Mountain Diner Griddle Cakes (1938)

4 cups white flour
2 tsps cream of tartar
1 tsp baking soda
2/3 tsp salt
1/4 cup yellow cornmeal
2 cups milk
2 tblsps molasses (light or
    dark, your choice)
1 egg, beaten

1. Sift flour, cream of tartar, baking soda, salt, and cornmeal together.

2. Beat milk, molasses, and egg together. Mixture should be the consistency of heavy cream. If necessary, add small splashes of water to correct thickness.

3. See Indiana Buckwheat Cakes for cooking method.

Georgia's Fried Cornmeal Mush

1 cup cornmeal
3 cups cold water, divided
1 tsp salt
2 beaten eggs
4 tblsps vegetable oil,
    divided

START THIS RECIPE the day before you want to serve it.

1. In a small bowl mix cornmeal with 1 cup water.

2. In a saucepan bring remaining water and salt to a boil and gently stir in cornmeal mixture a little at a time.

3. When mixture returns to a boil, cover and simmer over low heat until thickened, about 20 minutes.

4. Pour into a lightly greased bread loaf pan and refrigerate overnight.

5. In the morning slice the firm mush into ½-inch-thick sections.

6. Dip in beaten egg and fry in a heavy medium-hot skillet with approximately 1 inch of already heated oil. This old timey recipe calls for lard to do the frying. The flavor is definitely different, and better, but less sinful oils are okay.

7. Cook until crispy on the edges and light golden brown.

8. Drain on paper towels and keep warm in your oven.

9. Serve with your favorite topping—maple syrup, fruit syrups, jam, or preserves.

State Fair Blue Ribbon Cinnamon Buns

DOUGH

4 tblsps dry yeast
4 cups warm milk (approximately 105 degrees)
1 cup sugar
1 tblsp vanilla
4 eggs
1 tsp salt
1 cup oil
14 cups all-purpose flour

FILLING

4 tblsps cinnamon
1 cup sugar, divided
1/2 cup melted butter

1. In a very large bowl dissolve dry yeast in milk and sugar.

2. Add vanilla, eggs, salt, and oil. Mix lightly.

3. Begin to add flour a few cups at a time. *(The key to making this dough tender and light is to use as little flour as possible so the dough is as soft as possible. It should be right on the verge of sticky.)*

4. Turn out on a floured board and knead until smooth and elastic. Place dough in a warm, greased bowl and cover with a clean dish towel. Let it rise until double in size.

5. Preheat oven to 350 degrees.

6. In a small bowl mix cinnamon and sugar.

7. Roll out dough into a rectangular shape.

8. Spread evenly with butter and sprinkle evenly with cinnamon-sugar mixture.

9. Roll up dough and cut in 1-inch sections.

10. Place rolls on a cookie sheet and bake 15 to 20 minutes depending on how thick you cut the rolls and your oven's temperature.

New Hampshire Diner Griddle Cakes (1936)

2 tsps baking soda
2 cups buttermilk or sour milk
2 cups sweet milk
2 cups white flour
1 tsp salt
3 tblsps melted butter

1. Add soda to sour milk and stir well.

2. Add sweet milk.

3. In a separate bowl sift together flour and salt.

4. Thoroughly beat together milk and flour mixtures.

5. Add melted butter and beat once more.

6. Fry on a well-greased griddle at medium heat. See Indiana Buckwheat Cakes for more information.

Southern Style Corn Fritters

oil for frying
dash of black pepper
2 well-beaten eggs
1½ cups all-purpose flour
1 tsp baking powder
½ tsp salt
1 16-ounce can cream-style
    corn

1. In a small bowl combine salt, pepper, eggs and cream-style corn.

2. In a separate bowl sift together flour and baking powder.

3. Combine both mixtures.

4. Drop by tablespoonfuls into hot (350–375 degrees) oil or shortening.

5. Fry to a delicate brown and drain on paper towels.

6. Keep warm in your oven.

7. Serve with your choice of syrup or plain with butter.

Willy's Diner Pancakes

½ cup all-purpose flour
½ cup wheat flour
1 tblsp sugar
1 tsp baking powder
½ tsp baking soda
½ tsp cinnamon
¼ tsp salt
1 cup buttermilk or ¾ cup
    plain yogurt with ¼ cup
    water
1 large egg
2 tblsps vegetable oil
oil for frying

1. In a medium bowl sift together flours, sugar, baking powder, baking soda, cinnamon, and salt.

2. Add buttermilk, egg, and oil.

3. Beat until mixture is smooth.

4. Cook as described in Indiana Buckwheat Cakes.

Dixie Diner's Blueberry Waffles

2 cups all-purpose flour
2 tblsps cornmeal
4 tsps baking powder
$^1\!/_2$ tsp salt
2 tblsps sugar
1 cup milk
2 eggs, separated
4 tblsps melted shortening
1 cup blueberries or
    huckleberries

1. In a medium bowl sift together dry ingredients.

2. In a separate small bowl beat egg yolks and milk together.

3. Add egg mixture to dry ingredients and beat thoroughly.

4. Whip egg whites until stiff.

5. Add shortening.

6. Gently fold in berries and egg whites.

7. Bake in your waffle iron according to directions. Usually, this is to heat the iron, spray with nonstick spray (or you may have a nonstick surface), and cook for approximately 4 minutes. Waffles should be a nice golden brown.

8. Serve with a light-flavored syrup or white hard sauce. Provide a small bowl of extra berries to top off the waffle.

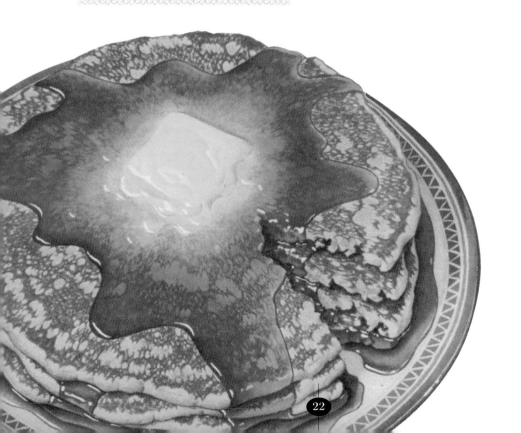

Lucy's Diner Golden Waffles

2 cups sifted all-purpose flour
3 tsps baking powder
2½ tsps sugar
1 tsp salt
2 eggs, separated
1½ cups milk
6 tblsps melted butter

1. In a medium mixing bowl sift together dry ingredients.

2. In a separate bowl mix together egg yolks, milk, and butter.

3. Make a hole in center of flour mixture and add egg-milk mixture. Mix just until moistened.

4. In a separate small deep bowl beat egg whites until stiff.

5. Gently fold egg whites into flour-milk batter.

6. Bake in your waffle iron about 4 minutes or until golden brown with crispy edges. I prefer my grandma's 1930s-era waffle iron that needs constant buttering and attention. For some reason these old cranky irons make the crispiest, tastiest delectable waffles.

7. For a bit of variety try pouring in batter and sprinkling with cooked sausage, bits of bacon, or ham. Plunk down the lid and inhale the wonderful aroma.

8. Serve your luscious waffles with any number of fruits, jams, maple or fruit syrup, or a yummy local honey from wildflowers.

Granny Glen's Biscuits n' Gravy

BISCUITS

1¼ cups all-purpose flour
2 tsps baking powder
½ tsp salt
¼ cup unsalted butter
½ cup milk
⅓ cup plain yogurt

SAUSAGE

1½ pounds lean pork
    sausage
½ tsp paprika
1 tsp dry sage
½ tsp salt
dash of black pepper
    (I prefer freshly ground)

GRAVY

4 tblsps butter
4 tblsps all-purpose flour
¼ cup water
2¼ cups milk

BISCUITS

1. Preheat oven to 425 degrees.

2. In a medium bowl sift together flour, baking powder, and salt.

3. Using your fingers crumble in butter until dough is the texture of coarse cornmeal.

4. Gradually mix in milk and yogurt.

5. Do not work the dough too much or it will get tough.

6. Turn dough onto a lightly floured board and roll out 1¼-inches thick.

7. Cut into 2-inch rounds with a biscuit cutter or floured rim of small glass.

8. Bake on a cookie sheet about 18 to 20 minutes, or until golden brown. Keep a close watch on them.

SAUSAGE

1. In a medium bowl mix together sausage, paprika, sage, salt, and pepper.

2. Shape into 8 small patties.

3. Place patties in a skillet (I hope you have a nice cast-iron one).

4. Cook over medium heat about 8 minutes per side.

5. Set aside and keep warm.

THAT YUMMY GRAVY

1. In the same skillet you cooked the sausage patties add butter and melt over low heat.

2. Scrape skillet to loosen sausage bits.

3. In a small jar with a lid or a similar plastic container, shake flour and water together until smooth.

4. Gently pour flour mixture into skillet, stirring constantly, until mixture becomes very thick.

5. Slowly pour in milk, stirring constantly, until gravy is smooth and the right consistency.

6. Serve over those yummy biscuits with a sausage patty on the side.

JoJo's Diner Special

3 tblsps butter
1/2 cup chopped onion
1/4 cup chopped green pepper
1/2 pound cooked, crumbled
    sausage
1 medium cooked, peeled,
    and cubed potato
1/2 tsp salt
dash of black pepper
dash of hot sauce
1/2 cup peeled and chopped
    tomato (canned, drained
    tomato is okay)
1/2 cup cooked chopped
    spinach
8 beaten eggs
1 tblsp parsley
1/4 cup Parmesan cheese

1. In a large heavy skillet melt butter over medium heat.

2. Add onion, green pepper, sausage, and potato. Heat and stir.

3. In a separate bowl mix salt, pepper, hot sauce, tomato, and spinach.

4. Gently stir in eggs.

5. Pour into skillet with sausage mixture; continue to gently stir and scrape off bottom of skillet until eggs are set.

6. Sprinkle parsley and Parmesan cheese over top.

7. Serve with more hot sauce, salsa, biscuits, or cornbread.

© Ronald Saari

Basic Omelettes

6 eggs
6 tblsps milk
$1/2$ tsp salt
3 tblsps butter
dash of black pepper

1. In a medium bowl beat together eggs, milk, salt, and pepper until blended but not foamy. Over medium-high heat melt butter in a 10-inch skillet. A good, well-seasoned cast-iron skillet is best.

2. When a drop of water bounces around in the skillet pour in egg mixture.

3. Reduce heat to medium.

4. As egg mixture sets, lift edges with your spatula and tilt skillet so uncooked egg mixture flows underneath. Do not stir.

5. Sprinkle on, or spoon on your choice of filling.

6. When eggs are set loosen edge of omelette and fold in half.

7. Slide onto a plate and serve.

FILLINGS

San Antone

$1/2$ cup cooked chopped chorizo
   sausage
3 tblsps chopped onion
$1/4$ cup chopped green pepper
   (a few pieces of red or
   yellow add color)
1 mild chopped green chile

Serve with salsa to spoon over the top.

Miss New York Diner's Omelette

$1/4$ cup cooked cubed ham
2 strips crisp crumbled bacon
$1/4$ cup cheese, your choice or
   a combination
$1/4$ cup chopped green pepper
$1/4$ cup chopped mushrooms
2 tblsps chopped onion

Fatty Patty's Country Omelette

$1/4$ cup crisp crumbled bacon
$1/4$ cup chopped onion
$1/4$ cup shredded cheddar
   cheese
$3/4$ cup cooked, peeled, cubed
   potatoes

Corned Beef Hash n' Eggs

4 tblsps butter
1 finely chopped small onion
1 pound chopped cooked
   corned beef
6 medium boiled, peeled,
   and cubed potatoes
8 eggs
dash of black pepper

1. In a medium skillet (I prefer a well-seasoned cast-iron one) melt butter and cook onion for about 1 minute. Don't brown it.

2. Add corned beef and potatoes. Press down gently.

3. As it begins to brown turn occasionally add pepper.

4. Make 8 wells in the hash and crack an egg in each.

5. Turn to low heat and cover. Cook about 3 minutes.

6. Serve with biscuits or cornbread. This makes as nice a dinner as it does a breakfast.

Red Flannel Hash

3 cups ground beef, pork,
   or a combination
4 cooked, peeled, and finely
   chopped medium
   potatoes
4 cooked, peeled, and finely
   chopped medium beets
1/4 cup finely chopped onion
1 tsp salt
1/2 tsp prepared mustard
dash of black pepper
4 slices lean bacon
1/2 cup cream or half and
   half

1. Preheat oven to 350 degrees.

2. In a medium bowl combine meat, potatoes, beets, onions, salt, mustard, and pepper.

3. Pat meat mixture into a 9-inch-square baking pan.

4. Top with the bacon.

5. Pour cream over all.

6. Bake 40 minutes or until cream is absorbed and bacon is crisp.

7. Cut into squares and serve.

Suggestion: a nice poached or fried egg on top. You might also serve with salsa on the side and biscuits or cornbread.

Comfort Diner's Chipped Beef

boiling water
1/2 cup chipped beef
1/2 cup vegetable oil
1/3 cup flour
4 cups heated milk (I prefer
    substituting 1 cup with
    canned milk, half and
    half, or cream to make
    the sauce richer)
1 hardboiled chopped egg
paprika
1/2 tsp salt
dash of black pepper

1. In a small bowl or pan pour boiling water over chipped beef, drain well. Break into small pieces.

2. In a medium skillet heat oil and slowly stir in flour until thickened.

3. Remove from heat and slowly stir in milk until smooth.

4. Return to low heat and add beef, salt, and pepper.

5. Serve over biscuits or toast.

6. Sprinkle a little hardboiled egg over each if desired and lightly sprinkle with paprika.

Soups

Aaah! What could warm the body and soul better than a hot, plentiful bowl of soup? Slide into a comfy booth, the friendly waitress takes your order and soon you're inhaling the steam rising from a homemade bowl of your favorite. Perhaps you'd like an overflowing basket of crackers on the side, or maybe a couple of Dairyland Rolls or Jim Scarborough's Cornbread.

Famous for the care and effort they put into their food, most diners pride themselves on making every last kettle of soup from scratch. Some even make their own basic stock! All of this from recipes passed from generation to generation. Maybe this is why most diners are located in the chilly northeast. To this day they fill a need to chase away the wintry cold with a serving of thick Chick'n Soup with Homemade Noodles from the Nook Diner or a hot, gooey grilled cheese sandwich accompanied by Creamy Tomato soup. *This* is true comfort food.

29

Nippy's Tomato Soup

2 tblsps butter
1/2 cup finely chopped onion
2 crushed cloves garlic
20 peeled, seeded, and
    diced Roma tomatoes
2 cups tomato juice
20 fresh finely chopped
    mushrooms
1/2 tsp freshly chopped
    rosemary
1/2 tsp freshly chopped thyme
1/2 tsp freshly chopped basil
1/2 tsp sugar
1/2 tsp salt
dash of black pepper
12 strips lean crisply
    cooked bacon
1/4 cup gin
1/2 cup half and half
1/2 cup chicken broth
1/2 cup sour cream
6 tblsps chopped parsley

1. In a large soup pot melt butter over medium heat and cook onions and garlic. Cook until onions are transparent but not browned.

2. Add tomatoes, tomato juice, mushrooms, rosemary, thyme, and basil. Cover and simmer 30 minutes.

3. Add a little more tomato juice if mixture gets too thick.

4. Stir in chicken broth, 1/2 cup sour cream, sugar, salt, and pepper.

5. Drain bacon on paper towels, crumble.

6. Add gin and bacon into soup, stir well.

7. Add half and half and quickly bring back to a boil.

8. Ladle into bowls and top with sour cream and parsley.

Skipper's Diner Soup

4 tblsps olive oil
³/₄ cup peeled, sliced carrots
2 finely chopped garlic
    cloves
2 cups peeled, cubed
    potatoes
2 quarts chicken stock
¹/₂ tsp dry thyme (1 tsp fresh
    is nice)
¹/₂ tsp salt
dash of black pepper
1 pound spinach, cabbage,
    or kale (your choice or
    combination)
1 pound Kielbasa sausage,
    cut into ¹/₂-inch sections
1 28-ounce can red kidney
    beans

1. In a medium saucepan cover sausage with water and boil 5 to 10 minutes. Set aside.

2. In a large soup pot heat oil over medium heat and sauté onions, carrots, and garlic until onion is transparent.

3. Add potatoes, stock, and thyme, salt and pepper to vegetables and simmer, uncovered, 15 to 20 minutes.

4. Wash and chop spinach, cabbage, or kale.

5. Add drained sausage and kidney beans and cabbage to soup pot and continue cooking another 10 minutes.

6. Serve with crusty sourdough bread, cornbread, or rolls to dip in broth.

Real Scotch Broth

1 cup whole dried peas
good beef bones (about 3
    pounds with some meat
    on them)
$3^1/2$ to 4 pounds lean beef
6 quarts water
4 large chopped carrots
3 medium chopped onions
1 small chopped head of
    cabbage
3 medium peeled and
    chopped turnips
3 medium peeled and cubed
    potatoes
1 tblsp parsley
1 cup large barley

1. Start this recipe the day before you want to serve it.

2. Soak peas overnight.

3. In a large soup pot place bones and meat; cover with water.

4. Bring to a boil, then turn down to simmer.

5. Add carrots, onions, cabbage, turnips, potatoes, parsley, barley, and dried peas.

6. Simmer 4 hours.

7. Run through sieve and serve with big crusty rolls.

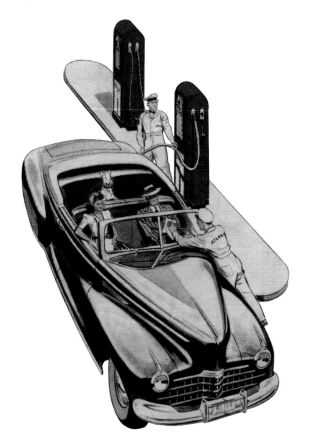

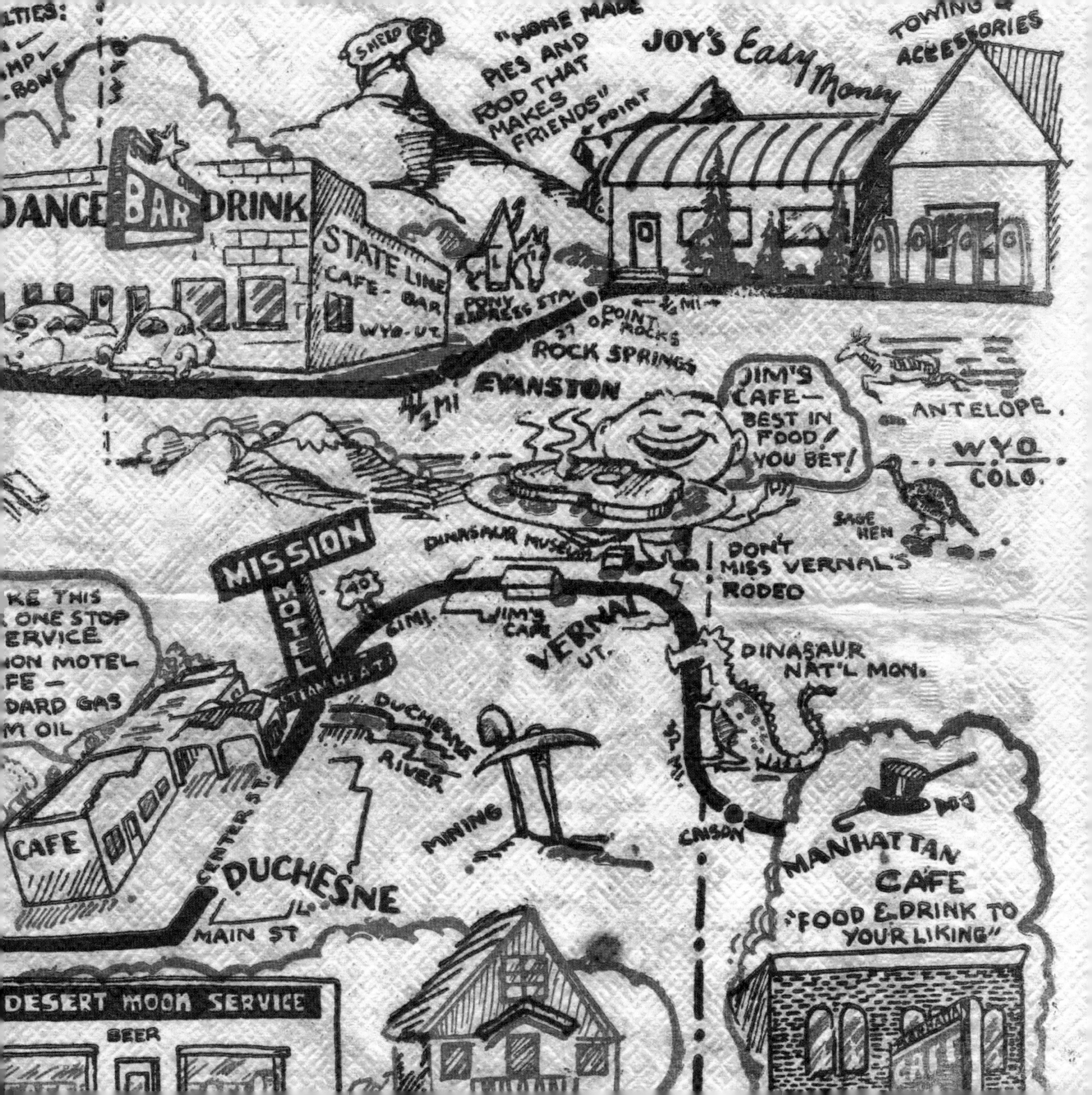

"HOME MADE PIES AND FOOD THAT MAKES FRIENDS"
JOY'S Easy Money
TOWING & ACCESSORIES
DANCE
BAR
DRINK
STATE LINE CAFE - BAR WYO-UT.
PONY EXPRESS STA.
POINT OF ROCKS
ROCK SPRINGS
EVANSTON
JIM'S CAFE — BEST IN FOOD! YOU BET!
ANTELOPE.
WYO.
COLO.
SAGE HEN
DINASAUR MUSEUM
DON'T MISS VERNAL'S RODEO
MISSION MOTEL
STEAM HEAT
40
JIM'S CAFE
VERNAL UT.
DINASAUR NAT'L MON.
DUCHESNE RIVER
MINING
CENTER ST
DUCHESNE
MAIN ST
CAFE
CARSON
MANHATTAN CAFE
"FOOD & DRINK TO YOUR LIKING"
DESERT MOON SERVICE
BEER

Neon Diner's Chick'n Soup with Homemade Noodles

1 3 to 4 pound chicken,
   trimmed of excess fat
   and skin, or equivalent
   in chicken breasts or
   thighs
1½ cups chopped onion,
   divided
1½ cups finely chopped
   celery, divided
dash of dried thyme
1 tsp salt
dash of black pepper
2 quarts water
2 tblsps chopped fresh
   parsley, divided
3 scraped and chopped
   medium carrots
1 10oz package frozen peas
   (optional)

1. In your large soup pot place chicken, ¾ cup onion, ½ cup celery, thyme, salt, and pepper with water.

2. Cook over medium heat 1½ hours or until chicken in tender.

3. While this is cooking make your Homemade Noodles (see page 35).

4. Remove from heat and pour through a sieve.

5. Pick meat from bones.

6. Skim as much fat from stock as possible.

7. Return meat to pot and add remaining onion, celery, 1 tblsp parsley, and carrots.

8. Bring to a simmer and cook 5 minutes.

9. Add Homemade Noodles and peas; cook 10 minutes longer. Garnish with remaining parsley.

10. Serve with your choice of French bread, Dairyland Rolls (see page 13), or biscuits (see page 10).

Homemade Noodles

1 cup sifted flour
1/2 tsp salt
1 well-beaten egg
2–3 tblsps milk

1. In a medium bowl sift together flour and salt.

2. Gradually mix in egg and milk.

3. Turn dough out on a lightly floured board and knead 5 minutes.

4. Cover with a clean dish towel and let rest 5 minutes.

5. Dust your rolling pin with flour and roll out dough into a rectangle about 1/8-inch thick.

6. Cut into strips about 1/2-inch wide and 6 inches long.

7. Separate noodles and let dry thoroughly before using.

8. Cook in your chicken soup broth about 10 minutes.

Split Pea n' Ham Soup

1 ham bone with meat on
it or 1 large ham hock
(as lean as you can
find); you might look for
smoked neck bones
8 cups water
2 cups dried cleaned green
split peas
1/2 cup chopped leeks
3/4 cup chopped onion
1/2 tsp salt
dash or two of black pepper
2 pared and chopped
medium carrots (some
people like 'em in their
split pea soup and some
do not)

PARKWAY RESTAURANT — 18 PARK AVE. W., MANSFIELD, OHIO

1. In a large soup pot put ham and water; bring to a boil.

2. Add split peas, leeks, onion, salt, and pepper.

3. Reduce heat and simmer 3 hours stirring occasionally.

4. Remove hambone and any loosened skin or bones.

5. Take all meat off bone and chop; return to soup.

6. Add carrots and continue to simmer 15 minutes more or until carrots are tender.

7. Garnish with croutons and serve with a green salad and crusty sourdough hunks.

Corn Chowder from the Sweetheart Diner

½ cup finely chopped
    salt pork
1 medium chopped onion
3 finely chopped potatoes
2 cups hot water
2 cups corn (fresh off the cob
    tastes best)
dash of black pepper
3 cups milk

1. In a soup pot fry pork until done.

2. Add onion and continue cooking until transparent.

3. Drain off any excess fat.

4. Add potatoes and water and simmer 25 to 30 minutes.

5. Add corn and pepper.

6. Add milk and simmer until soup is heated through. Do not boil.

7. Serve with nice Dairyland Rolls (see page 13) or, if you prefer sourdough chunks.

Roman Holiday Soup

2¹/₂ pounds good soup bones
    with some meat on them
4 quarts water
2 tsps salt
1 cup dried red kidney beans
³/₄ cup chopped onion
2 tblsps olive oil
1 cup pureed tomatoes (or
    equivalent in canned)
¹/₂ tsp coarsely ground black
    pepper
1 tsp crushed sage leaves
2 cups shredded cabbage
1 10 oz package frozen peas
4 tblsps chopped parsley
1 cup thinly sliced zucchini
¹/₂ cup dry macaroni
1 finely chopped garlic clove
¹/₄ cup uncooked white rice
    (long grain)
1 cup finely chopped celery
1 cup sliced carrots
grated Parmesan cheese

1. In your soup pot place soup bone, water, salt, rinsed and dried kidney beans. Simmer until meat is falling off the bone and beans are tender, about 2½ to 3 hours.

2. Remove soup bone, pick off any meat, and return meat to pot. Discard bone.

3. In a skillet heat oil and sauté onion until transparent.

4. Add onion to soup pot with tomatoes, pepper, sage, cabbage, peas, parsley, zucchini, macaroni, garlic, rice, carrots, and celery.

5. Simmer about 30 minutes or until macaroni, rice, and vegetables are tender.

6. Garnish with grated Parmesan cheese and serve with Garlic Bread (see page 65).

Creamy Tomato Soup

2½ cups peeled, quartered,
    seeded, and cooked
    tomatoes (or equivalent)
4 tblsps finely chopped onion
½ tsp salt
dash of celery salt
dash of baking soda
2 tblsps flour
2 tblsp butter
¼ cup cold water
2 cups half and half
sour cream
croutons
crumbled cooked bacon

1. In a large saucepot combine tomatoes, onion, salt, and celery salt.

2. Simmer gently 10 minutes.

3. Press through a fine sieve.

4. Return mixture to soup pot, add soda, and reheat on low.

5. In a small skillet melt butter.

6. In a small jar or other covered container shake together flour and water until smooth. Add to butter and stir until thick.

7. Slowly add half and half, stirring constantly, until smooth (about 1 minute).

8. Slowly blend flour mixture into soup.

9. Stir until soup is thickened. Be careful it doesn't scorch.

10. Pour into bowls and garnish with dollops of sour cream, croutons, or bacon.

11. Serve with crusty rolls or sourdough.

I like to serve this with grilled cheese sandwiches made with thick slices of Tillamook Cheddar™.

© Ronald Saari

Cream of Mushroom Soup from Harry's Midnight Diner

4 tblsps butter
1 cup chopped mushrooms
2 tblsps finely chopped
    sweet onion
2 cups chicken broth
3 tblsps flour
1/4 cup cold water
1/2 cup sliced mushrooms
1 cup heavy cream
1 tsp salt
dash of black pepper
crumbled cooked bacon
croutons

1. In your big sauce or soup pot melt butter and add chopped mushrooms and onions. Cook until onions are transparent.

2. Add chicken broth and bring to a simmer.

3. Mix flour and water in a small covered container; shake until smooth.

4. Gently stir flour mixture into soup.

5. Add sliced mushrooms, cream, salt, and pepper.

6. Continue to simmer, stirring often, 10 minutes more.

7. Garnish with crumbled cooked bacon or croutons.

8. Serve with sourdough rolls and a nice green or Caesar Salad.

Nor'easter Clam Chowder

1 quart (about 12) large
    rinsed clams
1/4 cup finely chopped salt
    pork (rind removed)
3/4 cup chopped onion
2 1/2 cups scalded milk
1 cup cream
3 cups peeled and cubed
    potatoes
2 tblsps butter

1. Drain clams and chop, save liquid.

2. In a large saucepot lightly brown salt pork over low heat.

3. Add onions and continue simmering 10 minutes more.

4. Add clams, milk, cream, and potatoes.

5. Simmer until potatoes are tender.

6. Stir in butter.

7. Serve with chunks of French or sourdough bread.

Sweet Stuff from the Counter

You've enjoyed a dinner of the consummate meat loaf with fluffy mashed potatoes and the waitress has taken away your plate. Your eyes slide over to the glass enclosed pie display and there beckons a piece of Banana Cream Pie, half a mile high and the answer to a pie lover's dream. Your waitress comes by, refills your cuppa joe and the next thing you know, that pie is yours. Or maybe your passion is a bowl of Peach Cobbler from Jake's, blessed with a scoop of vanilla ice cream or a mountain, (at least a *hill!*), of real whipped cream- yum! The choice is tough but you have to weigh the delightful pros and cons and remind yourself that there'll be another fine day when you can sit at the counter and luxuriate in one of your favorite diner's desserts. The recipes in this chapter will fill that craving for authentic diner goodies. Go ahead! Enjoy yourself! You deserve it!

Coconut Cream Pie

1/4 cup all-purpose flour

1 cup sugar

dash of salt

2 cups milk

3 beaten egg yolks

1 1/4 cups flaked coconut
(reserve 1/4 cup for top)

1 1/2 tsps vanilla extract

1 9-inch baked pie shell

3 egg whites

6 tblsps sugar

1. In a medium saucepan combine flour, sugar, salt, milk, and egg yolks.

2. Mix well and cook over medium heat, stirring constantly, until mixture is thick and bubbly.

3. Reduce heat and cook 2 minutes more.

4. Remove from heat and stir in 1 cup coconut and vanilla.

5. Pour hot filling into baked pie shell.

6. In a mixing bowl beat egg whites on high until soft peaks form.

7. Gradually beat in sugar until egg whites form stiff peaks and sugar is dissolved.

8. Preheat oven to 350 degrees.

9. Spread meringue over hot filling, making sure it covers all the way to the edges.

10. Top with reserved coconut and bake 12 to 15 minutes or until meringue is light brown.

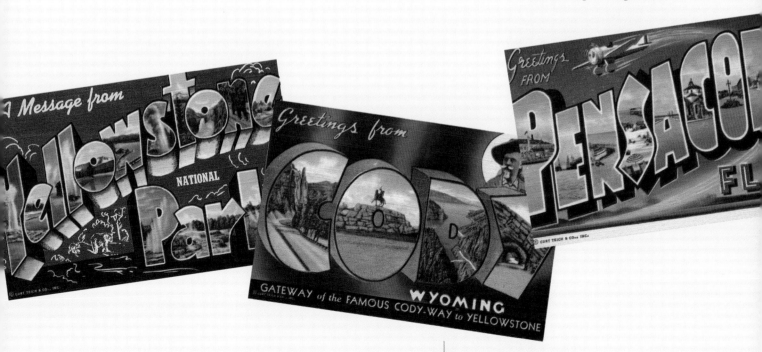

Banana Cream Pie

1. In top of a double boiler combine sugar, cornstarch, salt, and milk. Cook over boiling water until mixture becomes thick, stirring constantly.

2. Continue cooking and stirring another 10 minutes.

3. Stir about ¼ hot mixture into egg yolks, then pour back into filling.

4. Beat filling and cook 1 minute more.

5. Remove from heat. Add butter and vanilla.

6. Cool thoroughly.

7. Cover bottom of pie shell with about ¼ inch filling. Arrange banana slices in shell, cover with remaining filling. Add a thick fluffy layer of whipped cream. Chill before serving.

½ cup sugar

4 tblsps cornstarch

dash of salt

2 cups milk

3 slightly beaten egg yolks

1 tblsp butter

½ tsp vanilla

1 9-inch baked pie shell

3 ripe peeled, sliced
    bananas (peel should
    be flecked with brown)

whipped cream

Peach Cobbler from Jake's

about 6 fresh peaches,
   peeled, cut in slices or
   chunks
1/2 cup sugar
1 tblsp cornstarch or tapioca
1 tblsp lemon juice
1/2 tsp cinnamon
dash of nutmeg
3 tblsps unsalted butter
4 tblsps vegetable
   shortening
3 tblsps sugar, plus more for
   sprinkling on top
1 egg
1/2 tsp vanilla extract
3/4 cup all-purpose flour
1/2 tsp baking powder
pinch of salt
2 tblsps milk
vanilla ice cream or
   whipped cream

1. Preheat oven to 375 degrees.

2. Lightly butter a 9x12-inch baking dish.

3. In a medium bowl combine peaches, 1/2 cup sugar, cornstarch, lemon juice, cinnamon, and nutmeg. Stir well.

4. Pour fruit mixture into baking dish and dot with butter.

CRUST

1. In a medium bowl beat together shortening and sugar.

2. Add egg, vanilla, flour, baking powder, salt, and milk. Mix well.

3. On a lightly floured board roll out dough until rectangular and slightly bigger than the baking dish.

4. Roll dough onto rolling pin, roll out over peach filling, and seal around edges. Poke a few holes in the top and sprinkle a little sugar on top.

5. Bake about 1 hour or until crust is light brown and filling is bubbly.

6. Serve with a scoop of vanilla ice cream or whipped cream.

Butterscotch Pie (1940)

1/3 cup flour

1 cup firmly packed brown
    sugar

dash of salt

2 cups milk

2 tblsps butter

3 beaten egg yolks

1/2 tsp vanilla

1 9-inch baked pie shell

dash of salt

1/2 tsp vanilla

3 egg whites, room
    temperature

6 to 9 tblsps sugar

1. Preheat oven to 350 degrees.

2. In a small bowl mix together flour, sugar, and salt.

3. In a medium pan bring milk just to a boil.

4. Pour milk into top of double boiler.

5. Gradually stir flour mixture into milk and continue cooking until thickened (about 15 minutes).

6. Add butter and egg yolks and cook 2 minutes longer. Cool.

7. Stir in vanilla and pour mixture into pie shell.

8. Cover with meringue.

MERINGUE

1. Add salt and vanilla to egg whites and beat until mixture forms peaks.

2. Continue beating, adding 1 tablespoon sugar at a time until whites form stiff peaks.

3. Spread meringue over top of pie, being sure it covers edges.

4. Bake about 12 minutes or until meringue is light golden brown.

Mississippi Mud Pie-Lilly's Diner

2 cups crumbled chocolate
    wafer cookies
4 tblsps (1/2 stick) melted
    unsalted butter
1 1/2 cups sugar, divided
3 tblsps water
1/2 cup whipping cream
4 tblsps (1/2 stick) softened
    unsalted butter
4 ounces coarsely chopped
    semisweet chocolate
4 tblsps unsweetened
    powdered cocoa
4 tblsps (1/2 stick) unsalted
    butter
3/4 cup freshly brewed
    espresso
4 tblsps light corn syrup
1 tblsp coffee liqueur
1 quart softened vanilla ice
    cream
1/2 cup coarsely chopped nuts
    (macadamia, peanuts,
    almonds are especially
    good)

CRUST

1. In a small bowl combine crushed cookie crumbs with 4 tblsps melted butter.

2. Press crust mixture into bottom and up sides of a 9-inch pie pan with high sides, or use a springform pan.

CARAMEL SAUCE

1. In a small saucepan stir 3/4 cup sugar and water over low heat until sugar is dissolved.

2. Bring to a boil over medium-high heat and let boil until syrup turns a light brown. Do not stir.

3. Heat cream to just under boiling point (I do this in the microwave).

4. Remove pan from heat and carefully stir in cream.

5. Place saucepan on low heat and stir until well mixed and smooth.

6. Stir in 4 tblsps softened butter and set aside to cool slightly.

7. Pour mixture over cookie crust and freeze about 30 minutes.

FUDGE SAUCE

1. In a medium saucepan combine chopped chocolate, cocoa, 4 tblsps butter, and espresso. Stir over medium heat until smooth.

2. Add 3/4 cup sugar and corn syrup; increase heat to medium high and stir until sugar dissolves.

3. Increase heat until mixture comes to a low boil.

4. Cook sauce without stirring until sauce thickens, about 12 to 15 minutes.

5. Remove from heat and stir in coffee liqueur.

6. Cool sauce to room temperature.

7. Pour about 1 cup fudge sauce over the pie's caramel layer.

8. Return pie to freezer.

9. Set aside remaining sauce and keep just warm enough to pour.

FINAL PIE

1. Spread softened ice cream over espresso layer and return to freezer about 1 hour to firm up.

2. Pour remaining fudge sauce over ice cream.

3. Garnish pie with nuts and return to freezer about 2 hours.

Apple Pan Dowdy

1 1/2 cups sifted flour
dash of salt
8 tblsps melted butter,
    divided
5 to 6 tblsps ice water
1/2 cup butter
1/2 tsp cinnamon
4 tblsp sugar
dash of salt (again)
dash of nutmeg
10 peeled and sliced tart
    cooking apples
    (Pippin, Granny Smith,
    or Gravenstein are great.
    Try some of the new
    varieties)
heavy cream, ice cream, or
    cheese
1/2 cup light molasses

1. Preheat oven to 400 degrees.

2. In a bowl combine flour and salt.

3. Blend in 4 tblsps melted butter by crumbling in with your fingers.

4. Sprinkle with enough ice water just until dough leaves sides of bowl.

5. Roll out dough into rectangle and cut in half.

6. Butter dough, cut again in half.

7. Chill dough 2 hours.

8. Roll out dough again and divide in half once more.

9. Use half of dough to line a greased baking dish.

10. In another bowl combine sugar, cinnamon, salt, and nutmeg.

11. Top dough with apple slices and sprinkle with cinnamon mixture.

12. Combine molasses with 4 tblsps melted butter and pour over apples.

13. Cover all with remaining dough, seal edges, and poke two or three slits in top.

14. Bake 10 minutes, then reduce heat to 325 degrees for 1 hour.

15. Serve hot with heavy cream, good vanilla ice cream, or a nice slice of sharp Tillamook™ cheese.

PIE .... 20c   PIE A LA MODE 30c

—FROM THE FOUNTAIN—

MALTS (all flavors)	30c	COCA COLA	10c, 15c
MILK SHAKES	30c	ROOT BEER	10c, 15c
FREEZES	30c	BANANA SPLIT	40c
ORANGE	10c, 15c	LEMON-LIME	10c, 15c
SUNDAES	15c, 25c		

Seattle Diner's Blackberry Slump

1 quart washed and
    stemmed blackberries
1½ cups sugar
1½ tsps baking powder
1 cup all-purpose flour
½ cup milk
dash of salt
4 tblsps sugar
4 tblsps melted butter
whipped cream or vanilla
    ice cream

1. Preheat oven to 375 degrees.

2. In a greased baking dish pour in berries and sprinkle with 1½ cups sugar (less if your berries are extra sweet).

3. In a separate bowl combine baking powder, flour, milk, salt, 4 tblsps sugar, and butter.

4. Pour flour mixture over berries and bake 45 minutes or until crust is light brown and filling is bubbly.

5. Serve with freshly whipped cream or a scoop of vanilla ice cream.

Banana Cream Cake (1936)

1/2 cup vegetable shortening
1/2 tsp salt
1/2 tsp ground ginger
2 tsps vanilla, divided
1 cup sugar
2 unbeaten eggs
2 cups all-purpose flour
2 tsps baking powder
dash of baking soda
4 tblsps buttermilk
1 cup mashed ripe bananas
1 cup heavy whipping cream
4 tblsps powdered sugar
2 sliced ripe bananas

1. Preheat oven to 350 degrees.

2. In a large mixing bowl beat together shortening, salt, ginger, and 1 tsp vanilla.

3. Beat in sugar and cream well.

4. Add eggs, one at a time, and continue beating.

5. Sift flour, baking powder, and baking soda together and gradually add to sugar mixture.

6. Add buttermilk and mashed bananas.

7. Pour into two 8-inch well-greased layer cake pans and bake 25 to 30 minutes.

8. Meanwhile, in a deep bowl whip cream with powdered sugar and 1 tsp vanilla.

9. Allow cake to cool, then fill between layers with whipped cream and sliced bananas. Spread more whipped cream on top and garnish with a few slices of banana.

Caramel Raisin Pudding from Lizzie's Diner (1948)

2 cups flour
2/3 cup sugar
1/2 tsp baking powder
1/2 tsp salt
2/3 cup milk
1 1/3 cubes melted butter or
    margarine
1/2 tsp vanilla
1 1/2 cups raisins
1 1/2 cups firmly packed
    brown sugar
2 2/3 cups water (or fruit juice)
2 tblsps butter
vanilla ice cream or
    whipped cream

1. Preheat oven to 350 degrees.

2. In a large mixing bowl sift together flour, sugar, baking powder, and salt.

3. Beat in milk, melted butter, and vanilla. Mix well.

4. Fold in raisins and pour batter into 9x13-inch baking pan.

5. In a small saucepan combine brown sugar, water, and butter. Bring to a boil.

6. Pour brown sugar mixture over pudding batter.

7. Bake 30 minutes.

8. Top with a scoop of vanilla ice cream or a dollop of whipped cream.

Hot or Cold WE MAKE OUR

Knock-Your-Sox-Off Carrot Cake

2 cups all-purpose flour
4 tbsps yellow cornmeal
2 cups sugar
3 tsps baking soda
1 tsp baking powder
2 tsps cinnamon
3 large eggs
1½ cups vegetable oil
2 cups grated carrots
1½ cups flaked coconut
½ cup chopped dried apricots
2 tsps vanilla
½ cup chopped walnuts
¾ cube butter
1½ cups powdered sugar
1 8-ounce package softened
    cream cheese
1 tbsp lemon juice
¾ cup flaked coconut
½ cup chopped walnuts

1. Preheat oven to 350 degrees.

2. In a large mixing bowl sift together flour, cornmeal, sugar, baking soda, baking powder, and cinnamon.

3. In a separate small bowl beat together eggs and oil until smooth.

4. Add egg mixture to flour gradually.

5. Fold in carrots, 1½ cups coconut, apricots, vanilla, and ½ cup walnuts.

6. Pour into a greased and floured deep square pan and bake 60 minutes.

7. Let stand a few minutes to cool before frosting.

FROSTING

1. In a medium bowl beat together butter, powdered sugar, cream cheese, and lemon juice.

2. Remove cake from pan and frost when cool. Sprinkle ¾ cup coconut and ½ cup walnuts over top.

OWN CAKES *Delicious!*

Washington State Fair Apple Strudel

¹/₃ cup sugar

2 tblsps cornstarch

¹/₂ cup brandy or apple juice

2 pounds (about 5 cups)
    peeled and sliced tart
    apples (Granny Smith
    or Gravenstein are nice,
    but try some of the
    newer varieties too)

¹/₃ cup firmly packed light
    brown sugar

1 tsp ground cinnamon

dash of nutmeg

¹/₂ cup raisins

¹/₂ cup chopped walnuts

12 16x12-inch filo pastry
    sheets

1¹/₂ sticks (³/₄ cup) melted
    margarine

³/₄ cup dry white bread
    crumbs

3 tblsps powered sugar

1. Preheat oven to 375 degrees.

2. In a small saucepan combine sugar, cornstarch, and brandy or apple juice.

3. Cook over medium heat, stirring constantly, until mixture becomes thick and starts to boil.

4. In a separate bowl toss apples with brown sugar, cinnamon, and nutmeg.

5. Toss brandy mixture with apple slices.

6. Fold in raisins and nuts and set aside.

7. Unfold filo sheets and brush one sheet with melted butter. Sprinkle with bread crumbs. Repeat for each sheet. Layer sheets.

8. Spoon apple mixture across stacked layer and roll. Fold ends in before last roll to secure.

9. Cover cookie sheet with a layer of aluminum foil.

10. Carefully move roll of strudel to foil.

11. Brush strudel with butter.

12. Bake 35 minutes, or until dough is golden brown.

13. Serve with a thick slice of sharp Tillamook™ cheese, vanilla ice cream, or a dollop of whipped cream.

Betty Lou's Classic Rice Pudding

4 cups scalded milk

2 cup long grain rice

dash of salt

1/2 cup raisins (optional)

1 cup evaporated milk or
    heavy cream

2 slightly beaten eggs

1/2 cup sugar

1/2 tsp vanilla extract

dash of cinnamon

dash of nutmeg

whipped cream

1. In a double boiler mix together milk, rice, salt, and raisins.

2. Simmer over medium-high heat about 20 minutes. Stir occasionally.

3. In a bowl use a wire whisk to beat together evaporated milk or cream, eggs, sugar, and vanilla. Stir into rice mixture.

4. Cook, stirring constantly, 4 or 5 minutes more until thickened.

5. Pour into serving dish and sprinkle with cinnamon and nutmeg.

6. Spoon into individual dessert dishes and garnish with whipped cream.

Zinn's Modern Diner
Located on Route #222 — 12 miles from Reading
and 18 miles from Lancaster, Penna.

Salads n' More

What's a great sandwich without a heap of creamy Maynard's Potato Salad? Lonely! Or Masterful Meatloaf without a side dish of Sugar Baby Slaw? Pitiful! A serving of Walt's Tuna Melt without some of Priscilla's Pink Pickled Eggs? Gloomy! Salads are the partner, the complement, to all sorts of wonderful food. Whether it's the crunch and bang of a Basie Green Gids Salad with Cossack Dressing or the luscious flavor of Summertime Fruit Salad, there's a place for every style. Check out the recipes in this chapter to make your meal complete.

Sugar Baby 'Slaw

1 medium head of green
    cabbage
1 cup red cabbage
ice water
4 stalks finely chopped celery
6 thinly chopped green
    onions, with some of the
    tops for color
1 scraped shredded carrot
1 cup mayonaise
4 tblsps lemon juice
¼ cup sugar
dash of black pepper

1. Shred both green and red cabbages and cover with ice water. Chill 1 hour. Drain thoroughly.

2. In a large bowl toss together cabbage, celery, onion, and carrot.

3. In a small bowl mix together mayonaise, lemon juice, sugar, and pepper. Toss dressing with vegetables and chill before serving.

© Ronald Saari

59

Dizzy's Midnight Diner Bean Salad

2/3 cup vinegar
3/4 cup sugar
2/3 cup salad or vegetable oil
1 tsp salt
1/2 tsp coarsely ground black
    pepper
1 16-ounce can drained
    green beans
1 16-ounce can drained and
    rinsed red kidney beans
1 16-ounce can drained and
    rinsed garbanzo beans
1 16-ounce can drained
    yellow wax beans
1 16-ounce can drained and
    rinsed black beans
1/2 cup chopped celery
1/2 cup chopped green pepper
1/2 cup chopped red or
    yellow bell pepper
1/2 cup chopped sweet onion
    (Walla Walla or Maui
    are best)
1 16-ounce can pitted black
    olives

1. If possible, make this recipe the day before you want to serve it.

2. In a small bowl combine vinegar, sugar, oil, salt, and pepper; chill.

3. In a large bowl toss together beans, celery, onion, and olives. Add peppers.

4. Toss salad with dressing and if possible chill overnight.

5. Will keep in the refrigerator for 2 or 3 weeks if kept tightly covered and chilled.

Priscilla's Pink Pickled Eggs

1 dozen hard-boiled, peeled eggs, divided
2 tsps powdered ginger
12 crushed black peppercorns
3 finely chopped garlic cloves, divided
2 tsps pickling spices
2 cups vinegar
*1 cup water (use distilled if your water has chlorine or a lot of minerals in it)
2 thinly sliced sweet onions (use something like Walla Wallas or Maui if possible), divided
1 sprig fresh dill (or 3 tblsps dill seed)
1 cup juice from pickled beets

START THIS RECIPE 4 days before you want to serve it.

BRINE

1. In a medium saucepan put ginger, pickling spices, peppercorns, water, and vinegar. Bring to a boil and simmer 5 minutes.

EGG MIXTURE

1. Slice half of 1 onion onto the bottom of a clean crock or half-gallon jar with lid.

2. Add 1 clove garlic and 1 tsp dill seed or 4 heads of fresh dill. Add 6 eggs.

3. Continue layering onion, garlic, and dill seed with eggs, ending with onion. If necessary reheat brine and pour over all.

4. Refrigerate 4 days before serving.

5. These delightful eggs will keep for several weeks in the refrigerator.

6. If you like 'em hot you can add in a few hot chilies.

*Another method is to substitute 1 cup water with 1 cup juice from a can of pickled beets, which adds that bright color.

"Maynard's" Potato Salad

4 pounds small red new
  potatoes
1/2 cup mayonaise
2/3 cup sour cream
1/2 package ranch dressing
  mix
4 peeled and chopped
  hard-boiled eggs
2 thinly sliced celery stalks
1/2 cup finely chopped sweet
  onion
2 tblsps finely chopped red
  onion

1. Wash potatoes well.

2. In a large pot cover potatoes with water and boil gently until tender. Be sure not to overcook so potatoes won't fall apart.

3. Drain potatoes and let cool.

4. Cut potatoes into 1-inch cubes. Refrigerate.

5. In a medium bowl combine mayonaise, sour cream, and dressing mix.

6. In a separate large bowl gently toss together cooled potatoes, chopped eggs, celery, and onions. Toss with dressing.

7. Refrigerate 2 to 3 hours for flavors to blend.

San Fran' Salad

1. In a small bowl soak raisins in hot water; drain thoroughly.

2. In a large bowl toss together cabbage, apples, raisins, and peanuts.

3. In a separate bowl combine mayonaise, vinegar, and sugar.

4. Toss salad with dressing and chill.

1/2 cup raisins
1/4 cup hot water
1/2 large shredded head of
  cabbage
2 large peeled and chopped
  apples
1/2 cup chopped salted
  roasted peanuts
1/2 cup mayonaise
2 tblsps vinegar
3 tsps sugar

German Potato Salad from Fritzie's Diner

6 medium to large cooked,
    peeled, and cubed
    potatoes
1 cup lean bacon, divided
2 tblsps all-purpose flour
2 tblsps sugar
2/3 cup apple cider vinegar
1 tsp salt
1/3 cup water
1 tblsp celery seed
3 tblsps finely chopped onion
5 hard-boiled eggs
1 tblsp chopped parsley
    (optional)
1 cup finely chopped celery

1. Place potatoes in a large mixing bowl.

2. In a medium skillet cook bacon; drain on paper towels and set aside.

3. In remaining bacon fat (should be only a few table-spoonsful) add flour, sugar, vinegar, salt, and water.

4. Stir mixture until it thickens, about 2 minutes.

5. Toss bacon dressing with potatoes. Add bacon, celery seed, celery chopped and onion; toss gently.

6. Slice eggs horizontally and arrange around edge of bowl.

7. Garnish with a few crumbles of bacon and parsley.

8. Serve hot.

Fit for a King . . .

A MEAL WITH MAN APPEAL!

Basic Green Side Salad

½ small head lettuce
(try something other
than iceberg, or a
combination)
1 small sliced sweet onion
(Walla Walla, Maui, or
other mild variety)
¼ small sweet red onion
1 sliced small fresh zucchini
squash
1 grated medium fresh carrot
2 sliced stalks celery

1. In a nice salad bowl pull lettuce apart into bite-sized pieces.

2. Toss onions, squash, carrot, and celery with lettuce and offer one or more of the favorite salad dressings that follow.

3. Offer other garnishes such as pine nuts, croutons (see below), crumbled bacon, or other favorites.

Crispy Croutons

1 loaf thick sliced French
bread
⅓ cup virgin olive oil or 3
tblsps butter
1 large clove garlic, peeled
and crushed
½ tsp salt (optional)

1. Cut bread slices into ½–inch cubes.

2. Heat oil or butter in a heavy skillet at medium.

3. Add in garlic. Toss in bread cubes and gently cook, continuing to move and turn until croutons are light brown and crispy.

4. Drain on paper towels. Salt if desired.

Garlic Bread

1 large loaf crusty French
    or Sourdough bread
    (approx. 1 lb)
1 large or 2 medium whole
    cloves of fresh garlic,
    peeled
1 large or 2 medium ripe
    tomato(es)
3 tblsps olive oil (virgin or
    extra virgin according
    to taste)

1. Slice bread lengthwise.

2. Brush each half of bread with the olive oil.

3. Place oil side up on cookie sheet and toast under broiler for approximately 5 minutes (you want the bread to be light brown).

4. Slice off bottom of garlic clove(s) to get a nice fresh surface.

5. Rub garlic over both halves of the toasted bread.

6. Slice tomato(es) in half and scrub over the toasted and garlicked surface of the bread. Yum!

Cossack Dressing

1. Make this recipe the day before you want to use it, if possible.

2. In a small bowl blend together sugar and ketchup.

3. Add onion, oil, vinegar, pepper and salt. Mix well.

4. Refrigerate overnight if possible. Best when chilled.

1/2 cup sugar
1/2 cup ketchup
1 grated small sweet
    onion
1 cup salad oil
4 tblsps apple cider
    vinegar
1/2 tsp salt
dash of coarsely ground
    black pepper

Roquefort Dressing

2/3 cup half and half or
   evaporated milk
4–5 ounces Roquefort cheese
dash of coarsely ground black
   pepper
dash of salt (to your taste,
   some like more)
2 finely chopped garlic cloves
1 tsp celery seed
2 cups mayonaise
1 cup buttermilk
1/2 cup crumbled Roquefort
   cheese

1. In top of double boiler heat half and half or evaporated milk, 4–5 ounces cheese, pepper, salt, garlic, and celery seed.

2. Stir constantly until cheese has melted and mixture is smooth.

3. Let cool.

4. Stir in mayonaise and buttermilk. Mix well.

5. Gently fold in 1/2 cup cheese and refrigerate until ready to use.

Thousands of Islands Dressing

1. Start this recipe the day before you want to serve it.

2. In a small bowl mix together well mayonaise and chili sauce.

3. Add peppers and onion, mix in well. Refrigerate overnight.

1 cup mayonaise
4 tblsps chili sauce
3 tblsps finely chopped
   green pepper
1 tblsp finely chopped red
   pepper
2 tblsps finely chopped
   sweet onion

Summertime Fruit Salad

2¹/₂ cups available melons, scooped into balls

1 cup washed, stemmed strawberries, cut in half

¹/₂ cup blueberries

1 cup peeled, seeded, and divided citrus fruit (tangerines, oranges, tangelos, etc.)

1. In a medium bowl gently toss together all the fruits. Chill.

2. In a small bowl combine dressing and toss with fruit.

3. Chill at least 1 hour before serving.

Dressing

¹/₂ cup honey

dash of cardamom

¹/₂ cup water

1 tsp crushed mint leaves

¹/₂ cup sherry or port wine

JUST RIGHT FOR PURE DELIGHT !

CHEF'S SALAD BOWL

Selected Fresh Green Vegetables Topped with Cheese and Chicken Roll and Butter

Sandwiches at the Counter

Once sandwiches were all the original portable diner wagons offered, that and hot coffee. Workers getting off swing shift would find all of the "real" restaurants and cafes closed and dark. A thick sandwich of simple cheese or roast beef seemed like a T-bone steak to one of these dirty, weary laborers—and the price was right.

The sandwich has pretty much evolved and there are hundreds of varieties to tempt the palate. However, diners still preserve the tradition of the classics. Workmen still sit at the counter to eat a Blue Moon Diner Patty Melt, or Wednesday's Special B.L.T., but now they're joined by computer techies, the local banker, and maybe the artist who lives in a nearby loft. Before you know it, heads nod in hellos, elbows rest on the counter while everyone munches on their favorite sandwich, and someone begins to chat about the weather.

Off the Grill Ham n' Cheese

1/4 cup mayonaise

3 tblsps mustard (I prefer
   honey mustard or one
   with smokey flavor)

1/4 tsp horseradish (optional)

4 slices cooked ham,
   1/2-inch thick

butter

8 slices thick-sliced sourdough bread, divided

4 slices sharp Cheddar
   cheese, 1/4-inch thick

1. In a small bowl combine mayonaise and mustard (plus horseradish if you like it).

2. Spread mayonaise mixture onto each slice of ham.

3. Butter one side of each slice of bread.

4. Place four slices of bread butter side down on your preheated grill or heavy skillet. Temperature should be medium so you do not burn the bread before the cheese melts.

5. Top these slices with a slice of ham and cheese on each and cover with the remaining four slices of bread, butter side out.

6. As cheese starts to melt take your spatula and peek on the underside of the grilling bread. If it's brown, carefully flip the sandwiches.

7. Toast on second side.

8. Cut sandwiches in half and serve with your favorite side—coleslaw, potato salad, or baked beans.

Extra Special Grilled Cheese

1/4 cup softened butter

3 tblsps grated Parmesan
cheese

8 slices thick sourdough
bread

8 slices American cheese

8 slices Swiss cheese

1. In a small bowl combine softened butter with Parmesan cheese.

2. Butter one side of all slices of bread with Parmesan mixture.

3. Place four slices butter side down on your heated grill.

4. Top with cheese slices and top with four slices of bread, butter side out.

5. When cheese starts to melt, check bread for light golden brown color and gently flip over. Toast second side, cut in half, and serve with your favorite soup, side dish, or salad. I especially like this sandwich with the Nippy's Tomato Soup (see page 30).

Count of Monte Cristo Sandwich

3 well-beaten eggs

1 cup milk

dash of salt

3 tblsps melted butter

8 slices white bread

4 slices cooked chicken

4 thick slices Monterey Jack
cheese

4 thick slices Cheddar
cheese

1/4 cup oil
(vegetable is okay)

1. In a shallow baking dish combine eggs, milk, and salt.

2. Butter four slices of bread.

3. Top buttered bread with chicken and cheese slices.

4. Cover with remaining slices of bread.

5. In a skillet (I prefer cast iron) heat oil.

6. Dip sandwiches carefully in egg mixture and grill in skillet until both sides are golden brown.

7. Serve with a side salads or a light soup.

Blue Moon Diner's Patty Melt

1 pound lean ground beef
1/2 tsp salt
dash of black pepper
3 tsps vegetable oil
1 large thinly sliced sweet
    onion (the milder the
    better)
1 tblsp butter
8 slices thick rye bread
4 slices Monterey Jack
    cheese (thick sliced
    if possible)

1. In a mixing bowl combine ground beef, salt, and pepper.

2. Form into ½-inch-thick patties and fry in skillet about 4 minutes on each side. Set aside and keep warm.

3. Add oil to skillet and sauté onions until transparent. Be careful not to brown or they might become bitter.

4. Remove onions; set aside. Drain excess oil from skillet.

5. Butter one side of four slices of bread and grill in skillet.

6. Place bread on platter, butter side up, and top each with a 'burger patty, sauteed onions, and a slice of cheese.

7. Broil sandwiches 5inches from heat about 2 minutes. Cheese should be melted but not runny.

8. Top each sandwich with remaining slices of bread. Serve hot with a nice side dish like baked beans or potato salad.

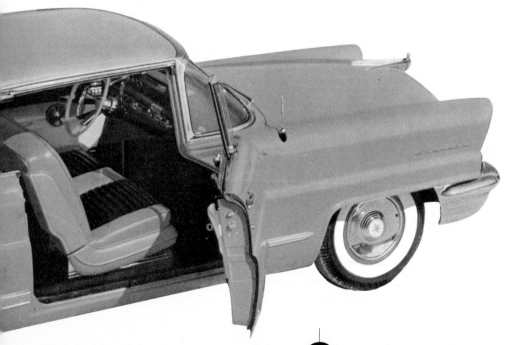

Walt's Tuna Melt

1 6-ounce can albacore tuna, drained
6 tblsps mayonaise
3 tblsps finely chopped sweet onion
3 tblsps finely chopped celery
1 tblsp finely chopped black olives
2 tsps lemon juice
$1/4$ tsp salt
dash of coarsely ground black pepper
4 tsps softened butter
8 slices thick sourdough bread
2 tsps grated Parmesan cheese
4 slices Cheddar cheese

1. In a small bowl flake tuna and combine with mayonaise, onion, celery, and black olives.

2. Add lemon juice, salt, and pepper.

3. Butter each slice of bread and sprinkle with Parmesan cheese.

4. Place four slices of bread butter side down in a cold skillet.

5. Top with tuna mixture and a slice of cheese.

6. Place remaining four slices of bread, this time butter side up, on top of tuna.

7. Grill over medium heat until bread is golden brown and cheese is melted.

8. Serve with your favorite salad or light soup.

Wednesday's Special B.L.T.

12 slices thick lean bacon
8 slices white bread
(be brave and try rye,
sourdough, or some-
thing wheaty and full
of seeds)
$1/4$ cup mayonaise
4 lettuce leaves
2 large ripe thick-sliced
tomatoes
3 tblsps butter (optional)

1. In that nice skillet fry bacon until crisp. Drain on paper towels and pat off as much fat as possible with more paper towels. Set aside.

2. Toast bread if you like it that way. Toasting keeps the bread from falling apart.

3. Spread mayonaise on four slices of bread.

4. Top bread with lettuce leaves, tomato slices, and three slices of bacon per sandwich.

5. If desired, butter remaining four slices of bread and top sandwiches. Some prefer a little mild mustard mixed with more mayonaise instead of using butter.

6. Cut in half and serve with potato salad or other favorite.

Night Owl Diner's Chili Dogs

2¹/₂ pounds lean ground
    beef
1 medium finely chopped
    onion
2 finely chopped garlic cloves
2¹/₂ cups diced tomatoes
    (canned is fine)
1 small can (¹/₂ cup) chopped
    green chilies
¹/₂ tsp salt
¹/₂ tsp black pepper
1 tsp ground chili powder
6 good-quality hot dogs
6 good-quality hot dog buns
    (the cheap ones just fall
    apart)
1 cup grated Cheddar cheese
¹/₂ cup finely chopped
    sweet onions

1. Brown beef in a skillet adding onion and garlic the last few minutes. Drain off any fat.

2. Add tomatoes, chilies, salt, pepper, and chili powder. Mix thoroughly. Simmer on low 1 hour.

3. Meanwhile, grill hot dogs until done.

4. Place hot dog on bun and spoon chili-meat mixture over top.

5. Sprinkle top with grated cheese and sweet onions; provide plenty of paper napkins.

6. Serve with some of those great baked beans and potato salad.

WONDERFUL!

SUCH FLAVOR!

SO TENDER AND JUICY!

SO EASY!

Chuck's Diner Chix Salad San'

1½ cups chopped cooked
    chicken
1 hard-boiled chopped egg
¼ cup mayonaise
½ cup finely chopped celery
dash of salt
dash of black pepper
1 tsp lemon juice
¼ cup softened butter
8 slices white bread
1 large thickly sliced ripe
    tomato
4 lettuce leaves

1. In a medium bowl combine chicken, egg, mayonaise, celery, salt, pepper, and lemon juice.

2. Butter four slices of bread and top with fair share of chicken mixture.

3. Top mixture with lettuce leaf and slice of tomato.

4. Finish sandwich with remaining slices of bread. Cut in halves.

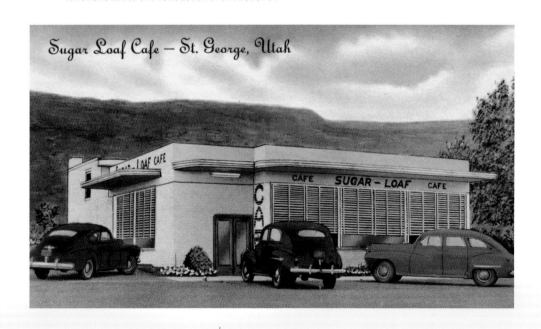

Sugar Loaf Cafe – St. George, Utah

Clucker's Egg Salad Sandwich

4 hard-boiled finely
    chopped eggs
3 tblsps mayonaise
2 tblsps finely chopped celery
1/4 cup sweet pickle relish
1 tsp mustard
1/2 tsp salt
dash of pepper
3 tsps softened butter
8 slices good quality white
    bread
1 medium sliced tomato

1. In a medium bowl combine eggs, mayonaise, celery, relish, mustard, salt, and pepper.

2. Butter each slice of bread and top with 1/4 of the egg mixture.

3. Top with a slice of tomato.

Tuna Salad San' at the Cozy Corner Diner

1 6-ounce can Albacore tuna,
    drained
1/2 cup mayonaise
1/4 cup sweet pickle relish
    (make sure you squeeze
    out most of the juice
    so your mixture is not
    sloppy)
3 tblsps finely chopped
    celery
3 tblsps finely chopped
    sweet onion
1/2 tsp salt
dash of black pepper
3 tblsps softened butter
8 slices good white bread
    (try this with sourdough,
    rye, or even a healthy
    multigrain wheat)
4 lettuce leaves

1. In a medium bowl flake tuna and combine with mayonaise, relish, celery, onion, salt, and pepper.

2. Butter four slices of bread and divide tuna mixture equally among them.

3. Top with lettuce leaf and the remaining bread.

4. Serve with your favorite side dish or soup. This is especially good with tomato soup.

© Ronald Saari

78

Hot Off the Grill

DEE-LICIOUS!

A diner owner once told me he took over the chore of washing dishes so he'd know what the customers really liked by what they left on their plate. In his case, it started out with the French fries. Soon, he was experimenting with this everyday accompaniment to make it a star of the menu. The key is to brown those tasty potato fingers according to the hungry diner's preferred degree of "brown-peas." Some like 'em light and golden, some like 'em suntanned like they've been lying on a beach a bit too long. Whatever your taste, this chapter includes not only the Real French Fry recipe, but savory delights such as Mushroom Burgers from Mooney's and more. Imagine stepping through that shiny stainless steel door at your revered corner diner and whiffing the smell of those French fries and burgers on the grill! Makes your mouth water!

All American Diner 'Burger

1 pound ground beef
    (do not use the extra
    lean; it cooks up too dry)
1 beef bouillon cube or
    1 tblsp granulated
    beef bouillon
1/4 cup finely chopped onion
1/2 tsp salt
dash of black pepper
4 slices American cheese
4 good-quality hamburger
    buns
4 lettuce leaves
1 sliced medium-ripe tomato

1. In a medium bowl combine well ground beef, bouillon, onion, salt, and pepper.

2. Shape meat mixture into four equal-sized patties.

3. Grill each patty about 5 minutes per side or until juices run clear.

4. Top each patty with a slice of cheese the last few minutes of grilling so cheese melts.

5. Toast buns on your grill.

6. Top bun with a patty, lettuce leaf, and slice of tomato. Cap off with remaining bun halves.

7. Serve with potato salad and baked beans, or Real French Fries (see page 81).

Real French Fries

8 large russet potatoes
peanut oil
salt

1. Scrub potatoes, peel, and cut into ¼-inch-thick strips.

2. Keep in cold water until ready to use.

3. In a deep fryer or heavy deep pot heat oil to 225 degrees.

4. Pat fries dry with paper towels and cook, a few at a time, in oil about 3 minutes. This is not to brown, but to blanch.

5. Dry fries on paper towels.

6. Turn up heat to 325 degrees and brown fries to desired color. Do not crowd.

7. Drain fries on fresh paper towels. Keep hot in warm oven. Sprinkle on salt before serving.

8. Serve with dipping sauce, ketchup, mayonaise (the European way), ranch dressing, or sweet n' sour sauce.

"Don't argue—just bring the ketchup!"

WELCOME TO *Frisch's* PADUCAH

✳DINE-A-MIKE®

does more & does it better!

DINE-A-MIKE IS THE FASTEST, MOST VERSA-
TILE, DEPENDABLE AND BEST PERFORMING
ELECTRONIC ORDERING SYSTEM AVAILABLE!
WE WILL PROVE IT WITH A DEMONSTRA-
TION AT YOUR LOCATION! CALL OR
WRITE TODAY.

✳DINE-A-MIKE®
DIVISION OF ELECTRONIC EQUIPMENT CORP.
2919 M St., N.W., Wash., D.C. 20007 • Area Code 202 FE. 8-6060

EVERY
DINE-A-MIKE
SYSTEM NOW
*Guaranteed
2 Full Years*

Mushroom 'Burgers from Mooney's

1½ pounds ground sirloin
¼ cup sherry
¼ tsp garlic salt
dash of black pepper
1 thick-sliced sweet onion
1 cup sliced fresh mushrooms
4 sesame 'burger buns
4 thick slices Monterey Jack
    cheese
1 peeled and sliced ripe
    avocado
1 sliced large ripe tomato

1. In a medium bowl thoroughly combine sirloin, sherry, garlic salt, and pepper. Shape into four patties. Fry patties in a heavy skillet until well done.

2. Remove patties to a platter and keep warm.

3. In the same skillet reduce heat and sauté onions and mushrooms until onions are transparent.

4. Lightly toast buns and place open on a platter.

5. Place a patty on each bun and cover with sauteed mushrooms and onions.

6. Top with slice of cheese, avocado, and tomato.

7. Serve with potato or bean salad.

Highway Diner's Chili-size 'Burgers

3½ pounds ground round,
divided

½ tsp garlic powder

3 tblsps vegetable oil

½ cup chopped onion

1 finely chopped garlic clove

½ cup chopped green bell
pepper

½ pound lean pork sausage

1 tsp salt

½ tsp chili powder

1 finely chopped large
canned green
chili pepper

1 1-pound can whole
tomatoes

1 1-pound can red kidney
beans

4 good-quality hamburger
buns

½ cup finely chopped
sweet onion

½ cup grated sharp
Cheddar cheese

1. In a medium bowl combine 2 pounds ground round with garlic powder and form into four patties.

2. In a heavy skillet, on high heat, sear patties on both sides.

3. Turn down heat and continue to cook patties 5 to 8 minutes more or until juices run clear. Set aside and keep warm.

4. In the same skillet heat oil and saute' onions, garlic, and bell pepper until onions are semitransparent. Remove to a bowl.

5. In the same skillet brown 1½ pounds ground round and sausage. Drain off fat.

6. Add salt, chili powder, chili pepper, tomatoes, and kidney beans. Simmer over low heat 30 minutes.

7. Add cooked onion, garlic, and green pepper. Simmer a few minutes more or until thoroughly heated. Stir often.

8. Place a cooked patty on half of bun and cover generously with chili mixture.

9. Offer chopped onion and grated cheese to sprinkle on top.

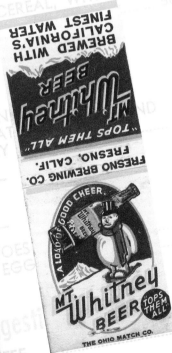

Blue Plate Specials

Somewhere is the story of why diners call their special-of-the-day "Blue Plate Specials." However, both diner aficionados and local clientele all know this means whatever delicious main dish the chef has decided to bless them with. Never demean the lowly meat loaf when it's made using the recipe from the Lander Diner, or scoff at chicken and dumplings as ordinary when trying this one here. The truth is, the polls show the vast majority of Americans still prefer good ol' comfort food like this. Basic and honest, you won't need a trip to the specialty market or a bank loan to put together these recipes. The final plus is the calls for seconds and the echoes of "yum!" from your family and friends.

Country Turkey or Chicken Pot Pie

2 roughly cut-up broiler-fryer
chickens, about 3
pounds each
water
3½ tsps salt, divided
⅓ cup butter or margarine
1 medium chopped onion
1 cup (about 2 stalks) sliced
celery
⅓ cup all-purpose flour
dash of black pepper
½ tsp crumbled dried thyme
(or 1 tsp fresh)
¼ tsp crumbled dried
rosemary (or 1 tsp fresh)
¼ cup butter or margarine
2 cups prepared biscuit mix
Bisquick™ or Krusteaz™
⅔ cup milk
1 pound cooked sliced
carrots (you can
substitute 1 can sliced
carrots)
1 10 oz package frozen peas
1 cup light cream or half and
half

1. In your large saucepan cover chicken with water, add 2 tsps salt, and cook until chicken is tender, about 45 minutes.

2. Scoop out chicken; set aside.

3. Put stock through a sieve and return to pot.

4. Add enough water to stock to make about 5 cups.

5. Remove chicken from bones and cut into 1-inch chunks.

6. Melt ⅓ cup butter in a medium saucepan and add chopped onion and celery. Sauté gently over medium heat until onion is transparent but not brown.

7. Add flour, 1½ tsps salt, pepper, thyme, and rosemary to skillet and stir until thickened.

8. Add this roux to chicken stock and cook until thickened and bubbly.

9. Stir often, then turn down to warm.

10. Heat oven to 450 degrees.

11. Cut ¼ cup butter or margarine into biscuit mix; stir in milk and beat about 15 strokes.

12. Turn dough out on floured board; knead several times and cut into strips or rounds.

13. Take thickened stock off heat and gently stir in chicken pieces, carrots, peas and cream.

14. In a large shallow baking dish pour in chicken mixture.

15. Cover with a lattice of biscuit dough strips or rounds arranged in rows.

16. Bake 15 minutes or until sauce is bubbly and dough is golden brown.

The Best Fried Chicken in the U.S. of A.

2 beaten eggs
1 cup buttermilk
1 cup flour
4 1/2 tsp salt
dash of black pepper
1/2 tsp baking powder
dash of paprika
1/4 cup yellow cornmeal
oil for frying
1 3-to-4 pound cut-up frying
    chicken

Dippin' sauce
1/2 8 oz can peaches with
    juice
juice of 1 lemon (about
    1/4 cup)
1/2 cup water (if needed)
3 tblsps brown sugar
1 tblsp butter
1 tblsp apple cider vinegar
dash each of salt and
    pepper

1. In a small bowl combine eggs and milk and beat.

2. In a separate bowl combine flour, salt, pepper, baking powder, paprika, and cornmeal.

3. Using your deep fryer or a deep heavy pot, heat enough oil to almost cover chicken. Oil should be at 350 degrees.

4. Dip chicken pieces first in egg mixture, then flour mixture, then back in egg mixture.

5. Gently drop battered chicken into hot oil. Do not crowd or oil will get too cool to form a crispy coating.

6. Move and turn pieces around. Turn over twice until well browned, each piece being turned twice, and juices run clear.

DIPPIN' SAUCE

1. Whirl peaches and their juice in your blender about 1 minute.

2. Add lemon juice, water (if needed to thin), brown sugar, butter, vinegar, salt, and pepper.

3. Pulse blender until all is well mixed but not foamy.

4. Serve as dippin' sauce for your fried chicken and also for French fries.

Countrystyle Chicken n' Dumplings

10 to 12 skinned chicken
    thighs, or equal in
    breasts or other pieces
3 tblsps oil
2 large sliced carrots
2 medium chopped onions
1 tsp salt
dash of pepper

1 drained 16-ounce can
    whole kernel corn
    (optional)
1 tblsp chopped fresh
    parsley
2 cups hot chicken broth or
    homemade stock
1 10oz frozen green peas
1 cup all-purpose flour
1/2 tsp salt
2 tsps baking powder
1 beaten egg
1/2 cup milk

1. Heat oil in large kettle or soup pot. Brown chicken a few pieces at a time.

2. Toss in carrots and onions and gently stir until onions are transparent.

3. Add salt, pepper, drained corn (if you like), parsley, and chicken broth. Simmer, uncovered, 30 minutes. Add peas just a few minutes before spooning in dumplings.

4. In a separate bowl mix together flour, salt, baking powder, egg, and about 1/2 cup milk. Dough should be moist but not sticky.

5. Spoon batter by tablespoonful into simmering chicken mixture, cover, and continue cooking 10 minutes. Do not lift cover while dumplings are cooking.

Dinner Pie from Jack's D.C. Diner

6 or 7 peeled and halved
new potatoes
water
1 tsp salt
4 tblsps butter, divided
dash of pepper
2 tblsps oil
3 chopped medium onions
1 grated large carrot
1½ pounds ground beef
1½ tsps rosemary
1 tsp salt
2 tsps Worcestershire sauce

1. Preheat oven to 425 degrees.

2. In a saucepan cover potatoes with water and add salt. Boil until tender.

3. Drain potatoes and mash with 4 tsps butter and the pepper.

4. In a medium skillet heat oil and fry onions until transparent.

5. Add grated carrot and ground beef.

6. Sprinkle with rosemary and stir meat often until browned and crumbled.

7. Add 1 tsp salt and Worcestershire sauce.

8. Butter an oven-safe casserole dish and fill with meat mixture.

9. Cover meat with mashed potatoes.

10. Dot top of potatoes with a little butter and bake 15 to 20 minutes or until bubbly.

Masterful Meat Loaf

$2/3$ cup dry bread cubes (about 2 thick slices of
white bread)

1 cup milk

$1\frac{1}{2}$ pounds ground beef

$1/2$ pound lean ground pork (unseasoned)

2 beaten eggs

$1/3$ cup grated onion

$1/2$ tsp salt

dash of black pepper

$1/2$ tsp ground sage

1. Preheat oven to 350 degrees.

2. In a large bowl soak bread crumbs in milk.

3. Add beef, pork, eggs, onion, salt, pepper, and sage.

4. Mix well with your hands and pat into a 9x13-inch loaf pan.

5. In a separate bowl mix together brown sugar, ketchup, dry mustard, and nutmeg. Pour over meat loaf.

6. Bake $1\frac{1}{2}$ to 2 hours, or until lightly browned and a butter knife inserted in center comes out clean.

7. If you have a meat thermometer, the internal temperature should be 180 degrees.

8. Serve with baked potatoes, mashed potatoes, baked beans, or green beans.

Topping

3 tblsps brown sugar

$1/4$ cup ketchup

1 tsp dry mustard

dash of nutmeg

Meat Loaf from the Lander Diner

2 pounds ground round
2 eggs
1½ cups bread crumbs
¾ cup ketchup
1 package onion soup mix
½ cup warm water
4 thick lean slices of bacon
1 8-ounce can tomato sauce

1. Preheat oven to 350 degrees.

2. In a large bowl mix together ground round, eggs, bread crumbs, ketchup, soup mix, and water. I use my hands to squish all this together well; no other method seems to work as well.

3. Put meat mixture into a loaf pan or form into loaf shape in baking pan.

4. Cover with bacon strips and pour tomato sauce over all.

5. Bake 1 hour. Drain off extra fat.

Sunday Meat Loaf from Val's Diner

2 eggs
1 cup milk
3 cups soft bread cubes
2 tsps salt
dash of coarsely ground
    black pepper (2 dashes
    if you like)
1 tblsp prepared mustard
2 tblsps finely chopped
    parsley
½ tsp basil
½ tsp rosemary
2 pounds ground round

1. Preheat oven to 350 degrees.

2. In a large bowl combine well eggs, milk, bread, salt, pepper, mustard, parsley, basil, and rosemary.

3. Add meat and mix well.

4. Shape into a loaf and place in baking dish or fill in loaf pan.

5. Bake 1 hour.

6. Goes well with baked potatoes, mashed potatoes, new potatoes, and buttered carrots.

281-1233
take-out service
dining room service
281-0017
banquet & catering

– Established in 1926 –

CLOSE COVER • STRIKE MATCH ON BACK

Home-style Meat Loaf

1½ pounds ground beef
½ pound ground lean pork
    or pork sausage
    (if necessary have your
    butcher grind up a
    couple of lean pork
    chops. Make sure this is
    not seasoned sausage)
2½ cups fresh bread crumbs
1 cup finely chopped onion
1 tsp salt
dash of coarsely ground
    pepper
⅓ cup milk
1 tblsp finely chopped
    parsley
¼ cup ketchup
2 tsp Worcestershire sauce
2 eggs

1. Preheat oven to 400 degrees.

2. In a large bowl combine well meats, bread crumbs, onion, salt, pepper, milk, parsley, ketchup, Worcestershire sauce, and eggs.

3. Press mixture into a greased (I use a cooking spray) 9x5x3-inch loaf pan.

4. Bake 50 to 55 minutes.

Quick trick for busy Saturdays!

Hoity-Toity Fancy Meat Loaf

1½ pounds ground round

½ pound lean ground pork (unseasoned)

2½ cups fresh bread crumbs

1 tsp salt

½ tsp coarse freshly ground black pepper

⅓ cup milk

1 tblsp dry crumbled parsley

3 tblsps ketchup

2 tsps Worcestershire sauce

2 tsps prepared mustard

2 eggs

3 tblsps butter

1 cup sliced onion

2 tblsps flour

1 tsp or 1 cube beef bouillon

⅓ cup Burgundy wine

1 cup water

1 3- to 4-ounce can sliced mushrooms, drained

1. Preheat oven to 350 degrees.

2. Combine meats, bread crumbs, salt, pepper, milk, parsley, mustard, Worcestershire sauce, and eggs in a large bowl.

3. Pack each section of large muffin tin about ⅔ full.

4. Bake 35 minutes and turn out onto platter.

SAUCE

1. In a medium skillet melt butter and sauté onion until tender.

2. Stir in flour.

3. Add bouillon, wine, water, and mushrooms. Stir until thickened and bubbly.

4. Spoon over individual meat loaves and serve.

REDWOODS

of CALIFORNIA

The Quintessential Meat Loaf

4 tblsps butter

1¼ cups finely chopped
onion

1 cup (1 medium) finely
chopped green pepper

2 finely chopped garlic
cloves

2 beaten eggs

½ cup beef broth or stock

1 tblsp Worcestershire sauce

1 tblsp hot sauce

1 tblsp soy sauce

1 pound ground round or
other lean ground beef

½ pound lean ground pork
(unseasoned)

½ pound ground turkey

1 cup finely crushed saltine
crackers

½ cup ketchup

5 thick-sliced lean bacon
slices, cut in half

1. Preheat oven to 350 degrees.

2. In a large skillet melt butter and add onions, bell pepper, and garlic. Cook, stirring often, until onion is transparent.

3. Remove from heat and cool slightly.

4. In a medium bowl beat together eggs, broth, Worcestershire sauce, hot sauce, and soy sauce until well blended.

5. In a large bowl mix (your hands work best) meats, onion mixture, egg mixture, and cracker crumbs.

6. Mix in egg mixture.

7. Shape into a loaf in baking dish or loaf pan.

8. Spread ketchup over top of loaf and arrange bacon on top of that.

9. Bake about 1½ hours or until juices run clear.

Lasagna from Lucy's Diner

Tomato sauce

2 sliced medium onions

2 finely chopped cloves of
garlic

3 tblsps olive oil, heated

3 cans (14.5 ounces each)
stewed tomatoes

3 cans (8 ounces each)
tomato sauce

3 cans (6 ounces each)
tomato paste

1 can (4 ounces) sliced
mushrooms

2 beef bouillon cubes

1½ cups water

¼ cup chopped fresh parsley

¾ tsp oregano

2 tsps salt

½ tsp thyme

1 tsp rosemary

dash of pepper

2 tblsps sugar

1. In your largest skillet sauté onions and garlic in heated oil.

2. Drain off any excess oil and add various tomatoes, mushrooms, bouillon, water, parsley, oregano, salt, pepper, thyme, rosemary, and sugar.

3. Simmer on low 2½ to 3 hours.

LASAGNA FILLING

1. Preheat oven to 375 degrees.

2. In your skillet brown ground beef and sausage together. Drain off any excess fat.

3. Add 1 quart of tomato sauce and stir well.

4. In a large saucepan or pot heat water to a boil and add oil.

5. Slip lasagna noodles into boiling water, stir gently, and cook until tender. Drain.

6. In a 9x13-inch shallow baking dish spread a little meat sauce and layer with noodles, then ricotta, then Mozzarella, more sauce, then Parmesan. Repeat until baking dish is full.

Lasagna Filling

1½ pounds ground
chuck

½ pound lean ground
pork sausage
(unseasoned)

2 quarts hot water

2 tblsps olive oil

10-ounce package
lasagna noodles

1 pint ricotta cheese

2 cups grated
Mozzarella cheese

1 cup grated Parmesan
cheese

7. Bake 30 minutes or until lasagna is hot and bubbly.

8. Cool 5 minutes, then cut into generous squares.

9. Serve with a nice green salad. My family likes Caesar salad alongside.

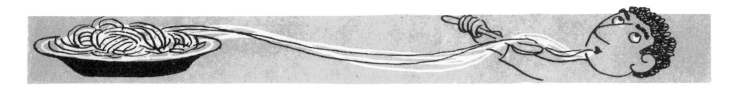

Fundraiser Spaghetti and Meatballs

Meatballs

1 pound ground beef
1/2 pound lean ground pork
(unseasoned)
1/2 cup dry bread crumbs
2 beaten eggs
2 tblsps water
3 tblsps chopped parsley
1 finely chopped garlic clove
1 finely chopped small onion
(about 1/2 cup)
1/2 cup grated Parmesan
cheese
1 tsp salt
1/2 tsp coarsely ground
black pepper

1. Preheat oven to 425 degrees.

2. Lightly grease a shallow
8x12-inch baking dish.

3. In a large bowl mix together
meats, bread crumbs, eggs, water,
parsley, garlic, onion, cheese, salt,
and pepper.

4. Form into 24 meatballs and
place in baking dish.

5. Bake meatballs 15 minutes;
turn meatballs in baking dish.

6. Bake 15 minutes more and
pour off any excess fat.

7. Reduce oven temperature to
350 degrees.

SAUCE

1. While meatballs are baking
make the sauce.

2. In a small bowl mix together
tomato sauce, wine or water,
oregano, salt, and pepper.

3. Pour over meatballs and
return to oven 10 minutes more
or until sauce is bubbly.

Sauce

1 15-ounce can chunky
tomato sauce
1/2 cup red wine or
water
1 tsp oregano
1/2 tsp salt
dash of black pepper
1 cup grated Parmesan
cheese

4. Serve over spaghetti and
sprinkle generously with cheese.

5. Great served with garlic bread
(see page 65) and a nice tossed
salad or Caesar salad.

Sunday Blue Plate Special at Rudy's
Beef Stroganoff

3 pounds boneless stew
    meat or round, cut in
    cubes
1/2 cup all-purpose flour
1 tsp salt, divided
dashes of coarsely ground
    black pepper, divided
1/4 cup cooking oil, divided
1/2 cup finely chopped onion
1 tsp paprika
1 1/2 cups beef broth
3 tblsps tomato paste
2 tsps Worcestershire sauce
1 tsp prepared mustard
    (Dijon or Dijon honey
    is best)
1/2 cup heavy cream
4 tblsps butter, divided
3 1/2 cups thinly sliced
    medium-size mushrooms
1 tblsp lemon juice
1 12-ounce package
    broad egg noodles
2 tblsps finely chopped
    parsley

1. Trim off all fat on beef.

2. Dredge meat in flour, 1/2 tsp salt, and pepper.

3. In a large skillet or sauté pan heat 2 tblsps oil and brown meat a few pieces at a time. Remove meat to a bowl.

4. Add remaining oil and sauté onions over low heat. Stir often and cook until just transparent, but not browned.

5. Add beef broth and scrape bottom of pan to release meat flavor.

6. Add meat and bring to a boil.

7. Turn down heat and simmer until tender, about 30 minutes.

8. Add paprika, broth, tomato paste, Worcestershire sauce, mustard, and cream.

9. Bring to a simmer, but do not boil.

10. In a separate skillet melt 2 tblsps butter and sauté mushrooms. Add lemon juice and mushroom mixture to meat and sauce. Keep warm.

11. In a large pot bring water to boil with 2 tblsps butter.

12. Add noodles and turn down heat to medium. Cook until tender.

13. Drain noodles and serve with meat sauce over top.

14. Sprinkle parsley over all.

Company Baked Ham with Glaze

1 12- to14-pound precooked
    smoked ham
20 whole cloves
1½ cups firmly packed light
    brown sugar
1 tblsp prepared mustard
½ cup orange marmalade
1½ cups apple juice
¼ to ½ cup bourbon

1. Preheat oven to 300 degrees.

2. Trim as much fat off ham as possible.

3. Score ham by cutting in ¼-inch deep slashes (through the skin) to make diamond shapes.

4. Using your sharp knife make 20 tiny slits all over ham and poke a whole clove in each slit.

5. Place on rack in an oven pan to drain off fat as ham cooks.

GLAZE

1. In a small bowl combine brown sugar and mustard.

2. Add enough marmalade to make a thick paste.

3. Spread glaze over ham (a small new paint brush works well). Be careful not to disturb cloves.

4. In a small bowl combine apple juice with bourbon and pour into roasting pan.

5. Cover with foil and bake 2 hours. Baste occasionally with glaze in pan.

6. Increase oven temperature to 450 degrees.

7. Remove foil and bake another 15 or 20 minutes. Baste often.

8. Glaze should become brown and thick.

9. Cool a few minutes, remove cloves, slice.

Zippy's Hungarian Goulash

1/4 cup all-purpose flour
1 tsp salt
dash of black pepper
2 tsps paprika
3 pounds lean chuck or stew
    meat, cut into cubes
3 tblsps cooking oil
1 1/2 cups chopped onions
1 smashed clove of garlic
1/2 cup water
1 20-ounce can chopped
    tomatoes
1/2 tsp salt
dash of black pepper
1 bay leaf
1 1/2 tsps caraway seeds
1 1/2 packages (12 ounces
    each) noodles
1 cup sour cream
4 tblsps butter or margarine
dash paprika and parsley
    (optional)
1 10 1/2-ounce can beef broth
    or equivalent in stock

1. In a small bowl or paper bag mix together flour, salt, pepper, and paprika. Toss meat in bag to coat well. Save 3 tblsps flour mixture.

2. In a heavy pot or Dutch oven heat all oil and brown meat on all sides.

3. Set aside meat.

4. Sauté onions and garlic in remaining oil from Dutch oven until onions are transparent.

5. Add browned meat, beef broth, tomatoes, salt, pepper, bay leaf, and caraway seeds.

6. Cover and simmer 2 hours, stirring occasionally.

7. 15 minutes before meat mixture is done, boil water in a large pot and add noodles. Cook until tender.

8. Remove bay leaf.

9. In a separate small bowl stir in sour cream and heat, but do not boil.

10. Toss noodles with butter and serve immediately with goulash spooned over the top.

11. Garnish with a little paprika and parsley if you like.

St. Patty's Day Corned Beef and Cabbage

6 pounds corned beef
water to cover
2 chopped medium-size
    onions
4 whole cloves
6 peppercorns
2 bay leaves
1 clove garlic
1 pared carrot
1 stalk celery
1 large head of cabbage

Zippy Sauce
4 tblsps butter
4 tblsps all-purpose flour
1 tsp salt
2 cups milk
1/2 cup prepared horseradish
1 tblsp lemon juice

1. In a deep kettle place corned beef and cover with water. Simmer 1 hour. Skim off any scum.

2. Pour off water; cover with fresh water.

3. Add onions, cloves, peppercorns, bay leaves, garlic, carrot, and celery.

4. Cover and simmer 3 to 4 hours or until meat is tender.

5. Cut cabbage into 6 wedges and place on top of meat. Cover and simmer until tender, about 15 minutes.

6. Remove cabbage with slotted spoon and keep warm.

7. Slice corned beef and serve with cabbage.

8. Offer mustard or Horseradish Sauce.

ZIPPY SAUCE

1. In a saucepan melt butter and blend in flour and salt until thickened.

2. Slowly pour in milk and stir constantly until mixture continues to thicken and becomes bubbly.

3. Remove from heat and stir in horseradish and lemon juice.

4. Makes 2 cups of sauce.

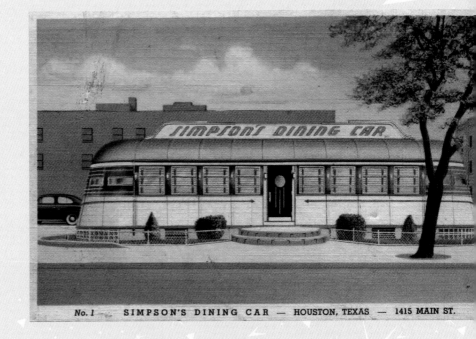

No. 1 — SIMPSON'S DINING CAR — HOUSTON, TEXAS — 1415 MAIN ST.

Nor'easter Crab Cakes

1 6½-ounce can crabmeat, or
    equal amount cooked
1½ cups soft bread crumbs
1 beaten egg
3 tblsps mayonaise
¼ cup finely chopped green
    onion
2 tblsps chopped fresh
    parsley
1 tsp Worcestershire sauce
dash of dry mustard
dash of hot sauce
2 tblsp butter or margarine

1. In a medium bowl place crabmeat with juices; flake with fork.

2. Add bread crumbs, egg, mayonaise, onion, parsley, Worcestershire sauce, mustard, and hot sauce.

3. Combine all ingredients well and shape into four 1-inch patties.

4. Melt margarine in your skillet and brown patties over medium heat on both sides.

5. Serve with your favorite salad or side.

Porcupines

1. In a medium bowl mix together rice, onion, green pepper, salt, black pepper, and ground beef.

2. Form into over-sized meatballs.

3. In a large skillet heat soup with water.

4. Add meatballs, cover, and cook on low about 50 minutes.

½ cup uncooked long
    grain rice
1 tblsp grated onion
2 tblsps chopped green
pepper
1 tsp salt
dash of black pepper
1 pound ground beef
1 can tomato soup
½ cup water

Meatballs from the Scandia Diner

1½ pounds ground chuck
2 envelopes onion soup mix, divided
2 cups soft bread crumbs
⅓ cup milk
1 egg
1 cup water
dash of allspice
1 tblsp flour
1 cup sour cream

1. In a medium bowl combine ground chuck, one envelope soup mix, bread crumbs, milk, and egg.

2. Shape into 24 meatballs.

3. In a large skillet brown meatballs and drain off any extra fat.

4. In a separate bowl combine one envelope soup mix, water, and allspice. Pour this mixture into skillet with meatballs.

5. Cover and simmer 20 minutes.

6. In a small bowl combine flour with sour cream and gently stir into meat. Heat thoroughly, but do not boil.

7. Serve over cooked noodles or rice.

Rosie's Truck Stop Stew

3 tblsps all-purpose flour
1 pound or so of lean beef
    (chuck works fine),cut
    into 1-inch cubes
2 tblsps oil
2 large onions, chopped into
    chunks
1 cup mushrooms, sliced or
    quartered, however you
    like
2 or 3 cloves of garlic,
    chopped fine
2 tblsp tomato paste
2 cans beef broth (or 2¹/₂ cups
    homemade or 2 bouillon
    cubes dissolved in 2¹/₂
    cups hot water)
3 cups thickly sliced carrots
    (about ¹/₂ inch)
3 medium potatoes (russets
    are best) cut into chunks
¹/₄ cup cold water
1 heaping tblsp flour
salt and pepper

1. Heat oil in a large heavy stewpot. Toss meat with flour and brown in oil over medium heat. Set aside.

2. Stir onions and mushrooms into pot with remaining oil (add a little if necessary) and stir until lightly browned, about 5 minutes. Add garlic and continue browning another minute. Pour beef back into pot and stir in tomato paste and broth. If needed add a little water to cover; bring to a low boil. Reduce heat to low and simmer until beef is tender, about 1¹/₂ hours.

3. Add carrots and potatoes. Cover and simmer 15 to 20 minutes (until potatoes are done).

4. In a small bowl mix together water and flour, making sure there are no lumps. Slowly stir mixture into simmering stew. Salt and pepper to taste. Serve with crusty garlic bread or chunks of sourdough.

Fancy Nancy's Meatballs

1 pound lean ground beef

1/2 pound ground turkey or
    chicken

1/2 cup onion, finely chopped

3/4 cup dry bread crumbs

1 tblsp parsley, minced

1 tsp salt

1/4 tsp garlic powder

1/8 tsp coarsely ground
    pepper

1 tsp Worcestershire sauce

1 egg

1/2 cup milk

1/4 cup vegetable oil

1/4 cup all-purpose flour

1 tsp paprika

1/2 tsp salt

1/8 tsp pepper

2 cups boiling water

3/4 cup cultured sour cream

1. In a medium bowl mix together beef, turkey, onion, bread crumbs, parsley, salt, garlic, pepper, Worcestershire sauce, egg, and milk thoroughly.

2. Shape meat mixture into balls a little bigger than a walnut.

3. Heat oil in a heavy fry pan.

4. Brown meatballs in oil, moving them around gently to brown on all sides.

5. Remove meatballs from pan and set aside in a warm place.

6. Mix together paprika, salt, pepper, and water, then add into fry pan. Gently stir until thickened, then slowly add sour cream. Stir until well blended, then add meatballs back to pan.

7. Turn heat to low and simmer 15 minutes.

No Squawk Chix Fried Steak

1 egg
2 tblsps water
1 tsp salt
1/8 tsp coarsely ground
  pepper
1/4 tsp paprika
1/4 tsp onion powder
1/4 tsp garlic powder
1 cup all-purpose flour
1/4 cup oil
1–1 1/2 pounds lean round
  steak, cut into four
  pieces

1. Beat together egg and water.

2. Mix together salt, pepper, paprika, onion powder, garlic powder, and flour.

3. Heat oil in a heavy fry pan over medium-high heat.

4. Dip steak pieces into seasoned flour mixture, then egg mixture, and repeat.

5. Brown steak on both sides.

6. Turn down heat, cover, and cook on low heat 20 to 30 minutes.

GRAVY

1. Remove meat to a platter.

2. Mix 2 heaping tablespoons flour with 2 cups milk.

3. Stir flour mixture into meat drippings and continue stirring until gravy comes to a boil.

4. Stir constantly 1 minute.

Alpine-Style Steak

2 pounds round steak (flank
    will work)
1/4 cup flour
1/4 cup oil (vegetable is okay)
1 medium onion, sliced thinly
2 1/2 cups cooked tomatoes
    (canned is okay,
    especially the garlic
    flavored)
1 tblsp Worcestershire sauce
1 tsp cider or white vinegar
1 clove garlic
1 tsp salt
1/8 tsp coarse ground pepper
2 tblsp brown sugar
3 tblsp ketchup

1. Flop that steak onto a cutting board and pound flour into both sides. You can use one of those mallets with teeth, or the side of a sturdy saucer will do, too.

2. In a heavy skillet (don't use cast iron because it will react to the acid in the tomatoes), heat oil and brown steak on both sides.

3. Add onion, tomatoes, Worcestershire sauce, vinegar, garlic, salt, pepper, brown sugar, and ketchup.

4. Cover and cook over low heat until tender, approximately 2 to 2½ hours. This can also be cooked in the oven at 300 degrees for the same amount of time. Remove cover for the last 15 minutes to allow sauce to thicken.

Americanized Swiss Steak

½ cup all-purpose flour, divided

1½ tsps salt, divided

½ tsp dry mustard

1 tsp Worcestershire sauce

¼ tsp coarsely ground pepper

1½–2 pounds round steak (okay, so we Yanks also use cheap chuck too)

3 tblsps oil

2 medium onions, sliced

2 cups tomatoes (canned is fine, home canned is better, fresh out of your garden is . . . well)

2 cloves garlic, minced

⅛ tsp coarsely ground pepper

½ cup water

1. Combine ¼ cup flour, 1 tsp salt, mustard, and ¼ tsp pepper. Spread half of mixture over steak and pound in with a meat mallet or side of a sturdy saucer. Flip over meat and repeat.

2. Heat oil in noncreative skillet and brown meat on both sides.

3. Add onions, tomatoes, garlic, and Worcestershire sauce.

4. Cover and simmer 1½ to 2 hours or until meat is fork tender.

5. Place meat on platter and cover with onions and tomatoes. Save juices.

6. Mix together ¼ cup flour, ½ tsp salt, ⅛ tsp pepper, and water until smooth.

7. Add to juices left in pan and bring to a boil, stirring gently until mixture is thickened.

Damn Yankee! Pot Roast

1/2 cup all-purpose flour,
    divided
2 tsps salt
1/4 tsp coarsely ground
    pepper
3- to 4-pound chuck pot roast
3 tblsps oil
1 cup water, divided plus
    more for pan juices
6 medium carrots, pared
    and cut in chunks
6 small onions (boilers are
    good) or 1 large onion
    cut into pieces
6 medium potatoes (or equal
    in small whites) cut
    into pieces
1 small turnip, pared and
    sliced (okay, so you
    hate turnips. Leave it
    out, but it does add
    richness to the juices
    and is traditional)
salt
pepper
1/2 tsp salt
1/8 tsp pepper

1. Combine 1/4 cup flour, 2 tsp salt, and 1/4 tsp pepper. Pat onto both sides of meat.

2. Heat oil in a Dutch oven or large skillet and brown meat well on both sides.

3. Add 1/2 cup water, cover tightly, and simmer 1 1/2 hours.

4. Add vegetables and sprinkle on a dash of salt and pepper. Add more water if needed to keep all from sticking.

5. Continue cooking until vegetables are tender, 35 to 45 minutes.

6. Remove meat and vegetables to a hot platter.

7. Skim fat from remaining juices.

8. Add enough water to pan to make approximately 1 1/2 cups of juice.

9. Combine 1/4 cup flour, salt, and pepper with 1/2 cup water. Mix until smooth. Add into meat juices and bring to a boil, stirring constantly until thickened. Serve meat with this gravy.

Big Daddy's Diner Meat Loaf

1½ pounds ground beef
½ pound ground pork
1 can (10½ oz) condensed
     cream of tomato soup
½ cup fine bread crumbs
½ medium onion, finely
     chopped (about ½ cup)
¼ cup green pepper,
     chopped
1 tblsp Worcestershire sauce
1 tsp salt
⅛ tsp coarsely ground
     pepper
1 egg, slightly beaten

1. Combine meats, soup, bread crumbs, onion, green pepper, Worcestershire sauce, salt, pepper, and egg in a bowl and mix thoroughly.

2. Use nonstick spray or oil on a 9x5-inch loaf pan and turn in meat mixture.

3. Bake in preheated 350-degree oven approximately 1 hour. Drain off any fat and let sit 5 minutes.

4. Remove loaf from pan, cut, and serve.

Mom's Meat Loaf

3/4 cup milk

1 1/2 cups soft bread crumbs

2 pounds ground beef

1 tsp salt

1/8 tsp coarsely ground
   pepper

1 small onion, finely
   chopped, about 1/4 cup

1 medium carrot, grated

2 eggs, well beaten

1/4 cup ketchup

3 tblsps brown sugar

2 tblsps prepared mustard

1. In a medium bowl pour milk over bread crumbs.

2. Add beef, salt, pepper, onion, carrot, and eggs.

3. Mix thoroughly.

4. Turn meat mixture into a 9x5-inch loaf pan that has been greased or sprayed with nonstick spray.

5. In a separate small bowl mix ketchup, brown sugar, and mustard. Spread over top of meat loaf.

6. Bake in a 325-degree oven 1 1/2 hours.

7. Drain off any fat and let sit 5 minutes before slicing.

Manny's Diner Fried Chicken

1/2 cup all-purpose flour
1 tsp salt
1/4 tsp pepper
1 broiler-fryer chicken
    (2 1/2 to 3 pounds) cut up
    or equal amount of fryer
    legs or thighs
about 2 cups oil (depending
    on size of your skillet)

1. Combine flour, salt, and pepper in a plastic bag. Shake a few pieces of chicken at a time in this mixture to coat.

2. Heat oil in skillet.

3. Brown chicken on all sides, turning often, about 15 minutes.

4. Cover tightly and continue to cook over low heat another 20 minutes.

5. Uncover and continue to cook 10 minutes. Remove to warm platter.

TO MAKE GRAVY

1. Pour off all but 3 or 4 tblsp drippings. Scrape crusty bits off bottom of skillet. Stir in 3 tblsps flour, 1/4 tsp salt, and dash of pepper. As it thickens add 1 1/2 cups milk. Stir over low heat until mixture is smooth.

Southern Smothered Chicken

1/2 cup plus 3 tblsps
    all-purpose flour,
    divided
1/4 tsp pepper
1 (5-pound) roasting chicken,
    cut up
1/4 cup butter
1/4 cup shortening
4 cups chicken broth

1. Combine flour, salt, and pepper in a plastic bag.

2. Shake chicken, a piece at a time, in bag.

3. In a heavy skillet heat butter and shortening over medium-high heat.

4. Brown chicken in skillet, making sure to turn often to brown all sides. Remove chicken, keep warm.

5. Pour off all but 3 tablespoons fat. Stir in 3 tablespoons flour and stir steadily until browned and thickened. Slowly add in broth, stirring until smooth.

6. Add browned chicken pieces, cover tightly, turn to low, and simmer 1 hour. May also be baked in a 350-degree oven for about the same amount of time.

This Ain't No Ordinary Meat Loaf!

1½ pounds ground beef

1 cup soft bread crumbs

²/₃ cup canned (drained), or
    1 cup fresh mushrooms,
    sliced

1 small onion, finely chopped
    (about ¼ cup)

½ pound Cheddar cheese
    (I prefer sharp), cut into
    1¼-inch cubes

¼ cup ketchup

1 egg, well beaten

1 tsp salt

⅛ tsp coarsely ground
    pepper

1. Combine beef, bread crumbs, mushrooms, onion, cheese, ketchup, egg, salt, and pepper in a large bowl. Mix thoroughly.

2. Turn into a 9x5-inch loaf pan and bake at 325 degrees 50 to 60 minutes.

3. Drain off fat. Let meat loaf sit 5 minutes, then turn onto an oven-proof platter.

Granny's Famous Hen Pie

1 (approximately 5 pounds)
    stewing hen
1½ quarts water
1½ tsps salt
1 small onion, chopped
1 carrot, cut in 1-inch pieces
1 clove garlic, peeled and
    smashed
1 stalk celery, chopped
½ cup all-purpose flour
½ tsp onion powder
½ tsp celery salt
3½ cups chicken broth
    (canned is okay), divided
dash of coarsely ground
    pepper
1 package (10 oz) frozen peas
    (optional)
basic pastry recipe

1. In a 6-quart stockpot place chicken, water, salt, onion, carrot, garlic, and celery. Cover and simmer until tender, approximately 3 hours.

2. Remove chicken and set aside to cool.

3. Combine flour, onion powder, celery salt and pepper with ½ cup chicken broth. Mix until smooth.

4. Heat remaining 3 cups chicken broth and bring to a medium boil. Slowly stir in flour mixture until smooth and thick.

5. Bone chicken and cut meat into bite-sized pieces. Add to gravy and peas.

6. Line a 9-inch-deep pie pan or baking dish with basic pastry (without sugar. Add a pinch of sage if desired). Fill with chicken mixture and seal top. Do not overfill. Save any leftover gravy to serve over pie.

7. Bake at 400 degrees 45 minutes or until browned.

Comfort Cafe's Chicken n' Dumplings

2 pounds chicken breast
2 quarts water
1 small onion, chopped
1 medium carrot, cut into
　　chunks
1 stalk celery, cut into pieces
2 tsps salt, divided
$1/2$ tsp coarsely ground
　　pepper
1 cup all-purpose flour
$1^1/2$ tsps baking powder
1 egg, beaten
$1/3$ cup milk
2 tblsps oil

1. In a 6-quart stockpot combine chicken with water, onion, carrot, celery, $1^1/2$ tsps salt, and pepper. Simmer 1 to $1^1/2$ hours or until chicken is tender.

2. Remove chicken from broth and cut into bite-sized pieces. Strain vegetables from broth and save.

3. In a small bowl mix together flour, baking powder, and $1/2$ tsp salt. In a separate bowl combine egg, milk, and oil.

4. Mix egg and flour mixtures together. Drop by teaspoonful into simmering broth. Cover and cook 15 minutes. Add chicken to reheat.

Steeltown Meat Loaf

1. Combine beef, sausage, oatmeal, onion, $1/2$ cup ketchup, eggs, 1 tblsp horseradish, salt, and pepper.

2. Turn into a 9x5-inch loaf pan and bake 50 minutes at 325 degrees.

3. Remove from oven and let sit 5 minutes.

4. Turn onto heat-proof plate or platter.

5. Mix together mustard, remaining horseradish, ketchup, and brown sugar. Pour this glaze over meat loaf and put back in oven 10 minutes.

1 pound ground beef
$1/2$ pound ground pork
　　sausage (regular
　　or sage)
$3/4$ cup dry regular oatmeal
　　(not instant)
1 medium onion, finely
　　chopped
$3/4$ cup ketchup, divided
$1/4$ cup milk
2 eggs, well beaten
$1^1/2$ tblsps horseradish,
　　divided
1 tsp salt
$1/4$ tsp coarsely ground
　　pepper
2 tsp prepared mustard
2 tblsps light brown sugar

Sunday Best Chicken from Lucy's Diner

about 2 cups oil or butter-
flavored shortening
(depending on size of
your skillet)
1 broiler-fryer, (2$^1/_2$ to 3
pounds) cut up, or equal
amount of fryer legs or
thighs, dried on paper
towels
$^1/_2$ cup flour
1 tsp salt
$^1/_4$ tsp coarsely ground
pepper
$^1/_2$ tsp garlic powder
$^1/_2$ tsp onion powder
$^1/_2$ tsp paprika
1 egg, well beaten
2 tblsps water

1. In a small bowl combine the flour, salt, pepper, garlic powder, onion powder and paprika.

2. In a separate small bowl mix together the egg and water.

3. Heat oil or shortening in a heavy skillet over medium-high heat.

4. Dredge chicken first in flour mixture, then in egg mixture, then again in flour mixture.

5. Fry pieces in hot oil for 30 to 40 minutes without lowering heat. The key is to keep moving and turning the pieces so they become crispy and brown without scorching.

6. As chicken gets done remove to drain on paper towels. Keep warm in oven until ready to serve.

7. Must be served with mashed potatoes and yummy country gravy.

Country Gravy
3 tblsps pan drippings
3 tblsps flour
1$^1/_2$ cups cream
$^1/_2$ tsp salt
dash of freshly ground
black pepper

COUNTRY GRAVY

1. Scrape the bottom of the skillet you fried the chicken in.

2. Stir in flour and mix with drippings, cooking over low heat until lightly browned and thickened.

3. Slowly add in cream and continue stirring until smooth.

4. Add in salt, pepper and simmer until heated through.

Buffalo Cafe's Spicy Chicken

12 or so fryer drumsticks or
24 drumettes
1 cup all-purpose flour
2 tsps garlic powder
1 tblsp seasoning salt
2 tsps coarsely ground
pepper
1 tblsp cayenne pepper
2 cups oil

1. Wash drumsticks and pat dry.

2. Mix together flour, garlic, seasoning salt, and peppers and pour into plastic bag.

3. Drop a few drumsticks at a time in the bag and fluff around until coated. Place on waxed paper or paper towels and let sit about 20 minutes.

4. Heat oil in heavy skillet on high. Drop in drumsticks when oil is hot (not smoking), making sure they do not touch. Crisp on each side about 15 seconds. Cover and lower heat to medium high.

5. Check often and turn chicken for about 15 minutes.

6. Drain on paper towels.

Chicken for the King

8 cups cooked chicken,
  cut into bite-sized pieces
1/2 cup sour cream
1 1/4 cups milk, divided
2 10-ounce cans cream of
  chicken soup
1/2 cup cornmeal
1 egg, lightly beaten
1/2 tsp salt
1/8 tsp pepper
2 cups Cheddar cheese,
  shredded

1. In a saucepan combine chicken, sour cream, 3/4 cup milk, and soup.

2. Heat until bubbly, stirring often. Spoon into 9x13-inch baking dish.

3. In a separate bowl combine cornmeal, 3/4 cup milk, egg, salt, and pepper. Mix well, then fold in cheese. Spoon over chicken mixture.

4. Bake at 375 degrees 20 to 30 minutes or until top is golden brown.

Potatoes Delmonico

10 small red potatoes
1/2 tsp salt
1/2 cup sour cream
1 cup whole milk
1 cup grated sharp Cheddar
    cheese
1/2 tsp dry mustard
dash of black pepper
Chopped parsley (about
    2 tblsps)
1/2 cup sharp Cheddar
    cheese for garnish

1. Preheat oven to 325 degrees.

2. In a saucepan cover potatoes with water, add salt, and gently boil until tender.

3. Drain and cool.

4. Peel and slice potatoes about 1/4-inch thick.

5. Arrange potatoes in a shallow baking pan.

6. In a mixing bowl combine sour cream, milk, cheese, mustard, and pepper.

7. Pour mixture into double boiler and cook over low heat until cheese has melted and sauce has a smooth texture.

8. Pour cheese sauce over potatoes.

9. Bake 1 hour.

10. Sprinkle parsley and 1/4 cup cheese over top.

11. Serve as a side to pork chops, steak, chicken.

Alabama Sweet Potatoes

6 medium sweet potatoes
1/2 cup milk
1/4 cup sugar
1/2 cup chopped walnuts
1/4 cup butter
dash salt
1/4 cup southern bourbon
marshmallows (optional)

1. Peel potatoes and cut in chunks.

2. In medium saucepan boil potatoes until tender.

3. Drain and mash potatoes.

4. Preheat oven to 350 degrees.

5. In a separate pan scald milk and mix in sugar, walnuts, butter, salt, and bourbon.

6. Add mixture to mashed potatoes and blend well.

7. Bake 30 minutes or until top is bubbly. If you top with marshmallows, bake until light golden brown.

8. Serve as a side to turkey or chicken.

Diner o' Rings

3 to 4 large peeled sweet
    onions (Walla Walla,
    Maui, or Visalia to
    name a few)
ice water
2 lightly beaten eggs
2 cups buttermilk
2 cups all-purpose flour
1 tsp baking soda
salt
cooking oil

1. Cut onions into ¼-inch slices. Soak in ice water until ready to fry.

2. In a separate bowl beat together eggs and buttermilk.

3. Add flour, baking soda, and salt to taste to egg mixture.

4. In a deep fryer or heavy deep pot, heat oil to 350 degrees.

5. Drain onions and pat dry with paper towels.

6. Dip onion rings into batter and fry a few at a time until golden brown. Do not crowd. Turn once.

7. Drain on plate covered with paper towels and season with salt to your taste while rings are still hot.

8. Keep warm in 200-degree oven.

9. Serve with your favorite dipping sauce—ketchup or ranch dressing.

© Ronald Saari

Conchita's Cornbread

1½ cups self-rising flour
3 tblsps finely chopped
    green pepper
2 tblsps finely chopped red or
    yellow bell pepper
1 well-beaten egg
1 cup canned corn
1 chopped jalapeno or other
    mild chile
¼ cup buttermilk
1 cup grated sharp Cheddar
    cheese, divided

1. Preheat oven to 400 degrees.

2. In a large bowl mix together well flour, peppers, egg, oil, corn, chile, and buttermilk.

3. Pour half of mixture into well-greased 4x13-inch baking pan.

4. Sprinkle half the cheese over batter, then pour remaining batter over top.

5. Sprinkle rest of cheese over top.

6. Bake about 25 minutes.

Elvis, State Trooper and reporters relax over a cuppa joe. 1956

Angelic Biscuits

2 packages active dry yeast
1/4 cup warm water
(between 105 and 115 degrees)
4 1/2 cups all-purpose flour
1/3 cup sugar
3 tsps baking powder
1 tsp baking soda
1 tsp salt
2 cups milk or buttermilk
3/4 cup shortening

START THIS RECIPE the day before you want to serve it.

1. Dissolve yeast with warm water in a small bowl.

2. In a larger bowl mix dissolved yeast with flour, sugar, baking powder, salt, baking soda, milk, and shortening.

3. Cover and place in refrigerator overnight.

4. Preheat oven to 375 degrees.

5. Roll out on floured board to about 1-inch thickness and cut with biscuit cutter or floured rim of small glass.

6. Place on greased cookie sheet and bake 20 to 25 minutes or until lightly browned.

7. Serve with preserves, jam, jelly, or local honey, or split in half and cover with gravy.

Index

Chicken

Desserts

Eggs

Pasta

Pork

Potatoes

Salads

Sandwiches

Blue Moon Diner's Patty Melt 72
Chuck's Diner Chix Salad San' 76
Clucker's Egg Salad Sandwich 77
Count of Monte Cristo Sandwich 71
Extra Special Grilled Cheese 71
Night Owl Diner's Chili Dogs 75
Off the Grill Ham n' Cheese 69
Tuna Salad San' at the Cozy Corner
    Diner 78
Walt's Tuna Melt 73
Wednesday's Special B.L.T. 74

Soups

Corn Chowder from the Sweetheart
    Diner 37
Cream of Mushroom Soup from
    Harry's Midnight Diner 40
Creamy Tomato Soup 39
Homemade Noodles 35
Neon Diner's Chick'n Soup with
    Homemande Noodles 34
Nippy's Tomato Soup 30
Nor'eastern Clam Chowder 41
Real Scotch Broth 32
Roman Holiday Soup 38
Skipper's Diner Soup 31
Split Pea n' Ham Soup 36

Maynard's Potato Salad 62
Priscilla's Pink Pickled Eggs 61
Roquefort Dressing 66
San Fran' Salad 62
Sugar Baby Slaw 59
Summertime Fruit Salad 67
Thousand Island Dressing 66